NATURAL *Wonders*

NATURAL Wonders

FINDING PEACE AND BUILDING
A FRAMEWORK FOR LIVING

BOB WILHELM

MAPLE SEED MEDIA
CHATTANOOGA, TENNESSEE

Natural Wonders: Finding Peace and Building a Framework for Living
© 2024, Bob Wilhelm. All rights reserved.

Published by Maple Seed Media, Chattanooga, TN

ISBN 979-8-9905005-1-8 (paperback)
ISBN 979-8-9905005-0-1 (eBook)
Library of Congress Control Number: 2024908212

bwilhelmideas.com

Publication managed by AuthorImprints.com

Between every two pine trees there is
a door leading to a new way of life.
— John Muir

CONTENTS

PREFACE

G rowing up, I believed that reality, at its core, was an epic struggle between good and evil. Supernatural forces existed beyond the natural world, not just outside it, but bigger than it. The clash of these supernatural primary forces was the essence of reality, and the rest, the everyday world, was the playing field for these outsized forces. Heaven and hell were opposing end zones.

Fear filled my imagination because these forces could be behind every odd occurrence, every strange sound at night or spooky scene. We were all engaged in this battle, and it permeated life. This is how I saw myself and the world growing up.

One afternoon, I had an insight that put this view to the test. As I was exiting a college class, an idea came to me that said, "How do we believe there is a supernatural if we do not know the limits of what is natural?" What is it specifically that nature can't do? Maybe we are too quick to accept a supernatural realm. Could it be that all phenomena are of the natural world? We just don't understand it all well enough yet.

For me, a lifelong and practicing Catholic, an active recruit in this existential battle of good and evil, this was tough to deal with. I was a believer. Thoroughly Catholic. My whole family was. I had wrapped up my identity in my faith and took the idea of a supernatural clash of good and evil as a given. But this new idea was so simple and sensible I could not ignore it. With this single idea, what used to be fine was suddenly a problem. Just like that, some of my most deeply held faith elements, my foundation, seemed contrived.

At first, I was unsure what to think about all this. I was afraid to talk about it because it was heresy. This was a dangerous, unholy idea, not something I felt free to share. My soul was at risk even thinking about it. Despite that guilt and fear, I knew that this insight was important to me. I needed to grab it and hold on to it. So, I wrote my ideas in a little journal.

Those initial words really changed my life, but not overnight. I kept that seed of a natural-focused philosophy a secret, one I privately cherished and nurtured. I stayed in this miserable middle ground for a long time, holding loosely to the faith of my youth, but thrilled at the possibility that I could grow past it.

A decade later, I returned to that notebook and developed those rough points into a little booklet I called *Good Consideration*. Writing that essay helped me sort out my conflict between the natural and supernatural views. It was a great step ahead. But even with many well-thought-out ideas on paper, I was afraid to share it with my family. This dissonance between my ideas and my actions was very painful. Growth is hard, conflict is inevitable, but I shied away from direct confrontation. Peacekeeper Bob, I kept that essay mostly on the shelf.

While I didn't discuss it much, I never stopped wondering. I continued to build out my beliefs. This search is personal and, for me, essential. Philosophy and the big questions of life have always been passionate interests of mine. I have spent so much time contemplating the topics of God, ethics, and how to live a good life. I hate to use the word "spent" because it implies I gave up something, that there was a cost. For me, it was not time spent but time happily engaged, pondering and critically evaluating deep and challenging ideas.

Now, in my late fifties, I decided it was finally time to tell my story and share my philosophical outlook. Filled with personal stories and fresh ideas, *Natural Wonders* is a memoir, but a philosophical one that explores these big life questions. Genuine and positive, it offers a philosophical framework that honors this amazing Universe of which we are a part. *Natural Wonders* is the story of my path through a painful part of my life, a period in which I was stuck between my old faith and appealing new ideas. I hope this encourages others who find themselves similarly stuck, no longer comfortable with long-held beliefs but unsure what to do next. There is a way to make progress with these big questions and hold on to reverence and wonder for the magnificence all around us.

1
NATURAL AND SUPERNATURAL

I pressed the metal handle, pushed open the door, and stepped outside onto the granite entrance-way. It was a beautiful spring afternoon at Siena College. My philosophy class had finished, and rich ideas about the Universe, God, and ethics played in my mind. I paused to take in the scene. Fresh spring air softly greeted me. Goldilocks would have loved it. With a few quick steps, I skipped down the stairs onto the path across campus toward my dorm. As I walked, I took in the trees, their big branches and more branches spreading out smaller and smaller. Leaves added various colors to the scene. High up, wispy clouds gave the sky depth. I floated on, ener-gized by the words spoken in class and the sweet feel at that hour.

With each step, I became more aware of everything around me. I entered the scene and became part of it. More than feeling a basic appreciation of nature,

I saw myself as a piece of it. I no longer observed it. I *was* it. Like a leaf, a branch, or a blade of grass, I inhabited this scene. I was part of a whole, a member of this club. The full expanse of everything was with me. This might have been unsettling. It might have made me feel small, being absorbed into my natural surroundings this way, but my dominant feeling that day was one of belonging.

Peace filled me. I felt more at ease with my existence and a sense of being adequate, fundamentally OK. Like the life surrounding me, I was all right. At a minimum, I had the same value as the trees, grass, and squirrels. I united with the natural world, and I felt like a better person because of it. Maybe I was not worse than the plants and animals around me. Ideas from class, still tumbling in my mind, fueled my shift in outlook. The air, light, and peace outdoors gave context. I saw no sinners in that scene. That scene included me. Wow!

Feeling not fully OK was how I saw myself growing up. We were Catholic, and I picked up a sense of guilt and inadequacy from those teachings. The priest and the liturgy subtly reinforced those views each Sunday morning during Mass. We were all sinners. God alone, through his love and forgiveness, could save us. Our flaws began with Adam and Eve, the forbidden apple, the betrayal of the only thing God required of us. Humanity had one thing to do, just one rule to obey, and we blew it. These first two people failed, and somehow their mistake became our burden, too. Besides original sin, we added to our unworthiness through our own sins. The burden of original sin weighed me down, and so did the shortcoming that I perceived in myself, in how I lived.

The path brought me between the library and the cafeteria, and I only vaguely noticed my surroundings. My glow continued. Ideas sparked through my mind. I entered the quad by the Hennepin dorm, then levitated up the three flights to my floor.

What expression did I have when I entered the room and joined my roommate? Was it a smiley daze, or a big-eyed stare like a surprised cat? Maybe it was a focused look, like a hawk, or a standing version of *The Thinker* statue. I probably wore an odd blend of all these looks, preoccupied yet peaceful.

This all must sound so cute or naïve, and I guess it might be, but this nature and philosophy communion I experienced was real. The natural world I merged with after class lifted me up so much, I had to write about it. I found a quiet place, looked around to be sure no one could read over my shoulder, and I opened a blank notebook. It was an undersized, spiral-bound notebook, comfortable, concealable.

From time to time, I wrote letters to my friends and family. I could bang out a term paper when I needed to, but writing philosophical or religious ideas, particularly doing so outside my coursework, was a new activity. Nervously, I turned to the first lined page and touched pen to paper. Before I knew it, words were flowing.

It was nature that came to mind first. The boundless and beautiful natural world touched me on my walk. That experience contrasted directly with the intellectual ideas of God that we read about and discussed in class. Leaning toward the natural, I wrote, "Maybe there is no supernatural." I asked, "How do we say there is a supernatural, or something beyond natural, when we do not know nature's limits? We don't know what, if anything, is beyond nature. What is it precisely that nature can't do?"

Before that day, I had never considered the words "natural" and "supernatural." Our class lecture did not specifically cover this topic. This idea somehow found me. It was something obvious that I had never noticed before and seemed so simple and sensible. Maybe the classroom ideas energized me. Maybe the beautiful weather that afternoon charmed me. Natural seemed plenty, and I was an equal part of it. So obvious. Why didn't I realize it before?

We know a lot about the natural world, but there is still so much left to learn. Could I acknowledge a supposed supernatural without knowing the limit to the natural? This was a solid question. We shouldn't make a supernatural claim until we have exhausted our understanding of what could be natural. This realization astonished me.

The pen zipped along. Words came quickly and easily, not a single cross-out. The points mattered, and so did the act of doing it. Writing my own philosophical views that day was a big step for me. I started genuinely thinking for myself about these topics.

Of course, I kept that notebook and still have it today, thirty-five years later. Below are my first words.

EVERYTHING IS NATURAL

There is a common distinction between *natural* things that are limited, or subject to the laws of physics, and *super-natural* things that transcend these laws. Supernaturals include God, ghosts (spirits), souls, heaven, hell, Satan, magic, miracles.

Throughout history, people have put the supernatural label on many occurrences they did not understand—for example, lightning, thunder, earthquakes, floods, fire. These all have the common thread of infrequence of occurrence, which makes them difficult to study and understand as well as a powerfulness which seems greater than us, awe-inspiring. If these are the characteristics that urge us to call something supernatural, we may make a bad assumption based not on knowledge but on our lack of it.

Maybe there is no supernatural. We simply don't know how these phenomena act and call them supernatural by default. Maybe every phenomenon is explainable according to the laws that govern them—we don't know these laws yet.

Not that the traditional "supernatural" things don't exist. All or some may exist, I don't know. But if they exist, we should assume they are natural until, by observation and study, we find they are not.

This is my assumption.

I was a little shaken after I wrote those words. I mean, I actually trembled. This was scary stuff. Did I, a lifelong Catholic, really mean to deny the supernatural? I paused and put the notebook away in my drawer to consider what was happening. Maybe this would pass, but no, the ideas stayed with me. The next day, I picked up where I left off and continued spilling my thoughts onto paper.

EFFECTS/RAMIFICATIONS

The traditionally supernatural things must be proven or disproven by natural laws. Once we know all the natural laws, we can do it. There seems to be no way to know whether we understand all the natural laws. Could be a dead end. However, we know some natural laws and therefore should pursue proving what we can by them. This yields an enlarging core of knowledge, and eventually the core will equal the circle.

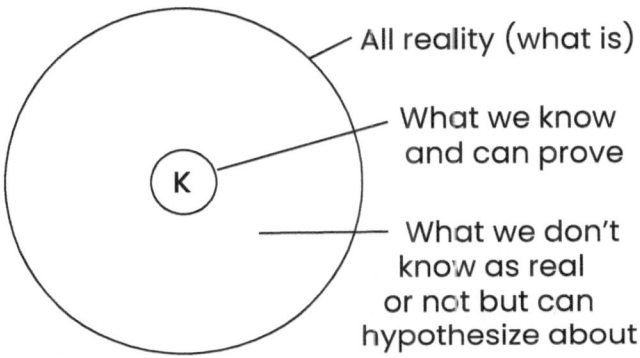

Eventually, all false hypotheses will be pushed out, leaving that part of reality we know, eventually, all reality.

With there being no supernatural things, or at least nothing we can call certainly supernatural (one must know the bounds of the natural world before one can label something as beyond the bounds), we must look for the principles that guide our life to be rooted in the natural—things our mind can reason about and find truth in.

This means that the problem of moral behavior should focus on things or circumstances our minds can know. We should not base morality on a supernatural goal but must tie it to and unite it with the object of our awareness. If morality, or any other principle, does not do this, it risks deceiving itself. More importantly, if deceived, there is no way of knowing it (proving it).

I was trying on the philosopher hat with those words. A little preachy, a little intellectual, and a little clunky, but my own. I also touched on a hopeful theme that it was possible to gain knowledge of how the world works. Over time, we can increase our understanding.

Nervous and excited, rebellious, I was a pioneer, and yet still, probably a sinner. I knew my thoughts were leading me into trouble. The ideas were 100 percent a clash with my Catholic faith.

My whole life I had been Catholic, and I liked it. I received the sacraments of Baptism, First Communion, and Confirmation. My grade school and high school were Catholic. For several years, I served as an altar boy. Even that walk after class took place at my Catholic Siena College. The Catholic faith was a deep part of who I was. Catholicism would not be all right with my doubting the supernatural. Was I a sinner for thinking this stuff? What was happening here?

Still, these notebook words were special. I produced something clear, simple, and reasonable. It was a statement about what one could say about God, the Universe, spirits, all the religious keystones. If they existed, they had to be natural. I knew those words clashed with the concepts of God, the devil, and other icons I owned for the first nineteen years of my life, but I did it anyway. When I pushed open the door and wrote the words that unfolded shortly after,

I made a 180-degree turn, a blind turn certainly, but a tremendous shift in my life's course.

What prompted this idea? Why did I start the notebook with those words? Could I not just hunker down and focus on my major, accounting, and get on with college living? Was something missing in my religious or philosophical outlook?

This idea sprouted in part because of timing. Put me, a naïve Catholic teen, into an environment brimming with ideas and respect for critical thinking. Pour on some philosophy classes, step outdoors into a full-volume nature scene, and boom, you get a reaction. The alchemy of circumstances that day helped sprout the idea, but there were three underlying factors that prompted me to write those natural and supernatural words. These three factors were my issues with the church, joy and wonder of the natural world, and inspiring philosophy classes.

ISSUES WITH THE CHURCH

As I grew from youth to teen, I lost confidence in the most foundational church teachings. While I loved being Catholic, I admitted to myself that not all the teachings made sense. The church doctrine of transubstantiation of bread and wine into Christ's actual body and blood bothered me. This most important aspect of the church's theology was always a stretch. I wished they intended the word symbolically, but no, they *meant it* as a factual change. This did not seem honest or reasonable. Why would the church require its members to believe something so clearly outrageous? Was this core Catholic faith tenet a test of loyalty to the church? One needed to stop thinking critically and profess this belief to show one's faith or loyalty. Yikes.

I remember one Sunday in church, as the ceremony approached the sacrament of the Eucharist, my discomfort rose. I looked around and thought, Come on, they're kidding. Don't they mean metaphorically, not an actual change? They mean *calling to mind*, or *reminiscent of*, the body of Christ, not a change to actual tissue, right? Ugh.

I wiggled in my seat, uncomfortable with this. I felt like an accomplice to a lie.

Prayer, also, did not sit right with me. Parts were fine. I loved prayers of thanksgiving. Whenever we said a prayer of thanks, usually with my loved ones, I always felt better. Even now, I like to express my thanks and appreciation to the Universe for my life, loved ones, and the world around me. I am so grateful, and prayer helps me own that feeling.

Prayers of petition were something else. With these, one wants something and calls for divine intervention to make it happen. The best petition-type prayers are well-wishes for significant outcomes like health or safety for someone else. The worst prayers are for petty things like for your team to win a game. Even with well-intentioned prayers, I didn't see how it made sense to ask God for something. Either God has our best interests at heart, or he doesn't. This is a juvenile example. But what would happen if some-one prayed for rain, but someone else prayed for sun-shine? Is it a contest of who prayed harder, whom God loves more? This all seemed like a game.

Over the years, my views on prayer have grown. I now think that even petition-type prayers have a place. These help us acknowledge what is truly important. They are our heartfelt pleas for who and what we love. This aspect alone makes a prayer of petition beneficial. In both prayer types, thanksgiv-ing and petition, the benefit is in the praying, not the outcome. The genuine gift of prayer comes when we say aloud, or under our breath, what matters most when we acknowledge who and what we care for.

I had a tough time imagining heaven and hell. These extreme afterlife outcomes were never comfortable. I liked the idea of reuniting with past departed rela-tives in heaven, but what age would I be there? Five? Thirty-five? Would my beloved pets be there? Hell is harder to grasp. I could never accept that some sup-posedly good God designed a noncompassionate sys-tem like that. Once, as a kid, I asked my dad after church about what the priest said, that we need to have a fear of God. Dad had little to say. He offered something about not wanting to anger God. Great, a God who can get emotional. Super.

I learned that there were inconsistencies in the Bible. These were usually minor, like different details in two versions of the same event. The Bible developed over time through stories told, retold, and written, translated, and rewritten over and over. Building the Bible was a circuitous and human process. As people developed the Bible, they made choices about what to include and exclude. Plus, the interpreter's biases, tastes, and skills influenced the translations. Translating is hard and subjective. Surely the Bible changed over the centuries. It developed as any human written book would.

It may surprise you, but I have spent many hours reading and enjoying the Bible. I often read the Bible in high school study hall. Regularly, I sat quietly in the auditorium balcony, our study hall, and flipped around randomly, searching for engaging stories to read. It sure beat studying. Those Bible stories told of ancient human dramas, life challenges, and moral choices.

I am a huge fan of Jesus. He exemplified compassion and love, and his life is inspirational. The descriptions of Jesus's interactions with others, particularly to the less powerful or society's outcasts, are great lessons. One can find meaningful lessons and inspiration in the Bible, and many of these are not of the supernatural but involve human choices and challenges.

The Bible guides us in valuable ways, but we should recognize that it is a book, a man-made book, and not base our philosophical or ethical views on it.

I did not hate the Catholic Church or find its morality overly confining. I liked it so much, but I couldn't reconcile the theology with emerging views that seemed more sensible. If I could have let these discomforts roll off, then I could have continued to enjoy the benefits of the church. Take it all with a grain of salt, some winks, and some nods. Just don't take it too seriously. This bothered me. If they say it is true, they should expect you to take it seriously. By my second year of college, these factors had put a meaningful crack in my faith.

THE NATURAL WORLD

Nature itself fostered those natural and supernatural words. Our family loved nature, and we spent lots of time outdoors. This was a big part of who we were. Nature was almost as much of an influence on me as our Catholic religiosity. This influence was more subtle than the church orientation, but it was real. Plus, we saw the divine in the grandeur of the outdoors. There was a connection, something meaningful or spiritual, we found in nature.

The single biggest dose of nature we enjoyed was on our annual car camping vacations in the Adirondacks. We stayed at two campgrounds over the years, Lewey Lake and Fish Creek Ponds. Woodland streams at both locations brought me so much joy. The first stream is the little inlet that joins Lewey Lake with Indian Lake. One day while camping at the Lewey Lake campground, my brother Jim and I prowled a canoe through those calm, marshy waters. Jim was a young man in his early twenties, and I was fourteen years his junior. Though close to our campsite, this stream felt so wild. I remember the clear water, lily pads, tall pines in the distance, narrow, reed-lined channels with a gently flowing current. Our canoe glided through the shallows. The summer marsh-land air was heavy around us. We sensed nature, got brushed by it, ducked under it, and took it all in.

Sometimes nature is expansive, as when you gaze over the ocean or from a mountaintop. Other times, it is close up and intimate. The scene in front of you shrinks to just feet or inches. All that grandeur gets condensed into a tiny area just off our fingertips. That was my experience in that canoe, nature close up and rich.

After a while, we eased out of the narrows into more open water. Jim steered as we paddled across the pond toward the far shore and landed the canoe in a place we had never been. There, our pleasant paddle journey became an adventure. Beyond the trees, we noticed a small cabin, and we walked together toward the shack. It looked quiet and unoccupied, but it was eerie. Jim opened the creaky door, and we stepped into a well-kept rustic camp but one with a stale air about the place. He asked me to stay on the ground floor while he explored. He walked around, then climbed the stairs to the second floor. His footfalls moved from room to room above me. I wanted to call him down and get us out of there. I held out, stood bravely. Phew! Jim returned all good, and we lived to canoe another day.

The second stream that captured my imagination was the waterway that connects Fish Creek Ponds to Floodwood Pond in the Adirondacks. This is a five-mile-long stream and a group of small lakes near Fish Creek Pond's camping area. The first segment by the campground is beautiful, with a mix of narrow and wider sections. The flowing water is dark, and branches overhead form a tunnel in places. Grasses drift in the current, and fish mingle among weeds. Occasionally, there is deeper blue water with small waves, as the river occasionally opens into bays and small lakes.

The state prohibited the use of motors about one thousand feet upriver. This is where the stream is most pleasing. Everything is quiet and unspoiled. Mom, Dad, and I visited Fish Creek Pond Campground for two weeks each year, but memories of our paddles up that idyllic stream stayed with me year-round.

Mountains appeal to me. They combine both grandness and intimacy. Grandness is in the stunning visual aesthetic, the remoteness of the peak, and the sweeping views from the top. Intimacy is in the hard physical work of climbing, the sweat and effort. Mountains have this personality about them. They call to you, but when you go to them, they push back on you with rocky trails and steep vertical ascents.

One day when I was about six, my family and I hiked up Saint Regis Mountain, also in the Adirondacks. I had a wonderful time outdoors with everyone. The view from the summit made me gasp. We sat around at the top, drinking water and chatting. I remember asking, "Why did we do this?" I wasn't complaining or grumpy, just inquisitive. Hiking up a mountain was something I wanted to learn more about. I loved it, but why did we hike it? Is this what adult people do? I eventually realized that experiencing nature directly, by panting and rock hopping on mountain trails, is inspirational. Effortful hiking links you to something undoubtedly real. When you hike a peak accompanied by your loved ones, it is even better.

When I was young, my brother Jim and I had another cool nature experience. This one we now call the Great Tadpole Transfer. Our home was in a growing suburb with new houses going up left and right. It was the early seventies, and we lived on one of the last developed streets in the area. As a child in this neighborhood, I played in the yards and rougher parts that were not yet yards and homes. Down the street were a few houses, then the road ended at a small pond. This pond was just the right size, easily walkable, but big enough to be interesting. Dad and I often took a small net and circled the pond in search of frogs, turtles, or other little wildlife.

The vegetation along the pond's edge gave cover to the little creatures. Every few steps along the bank, we came upon small openings in the branches and weeds. We moved like predators and crept up on those gaps. Maybe we would find eyes or a snout poking above the water's surface. These expeditions to the pond were our own local safaris. We explored there regularly in the evenings after his work and weekends too. We had so much fun.

This pond was also where Dad taught me to throw by making sure I stepped forward with my left foot. The pond had a huge rock at the far end. The base was in the water, but it stood out quite high. Imagining it now, let's call it ten feet above the water and five feet wide at its base. We'd throw small rocks at that big rock slab on the far side. Throwing has been a life-long joy, and this pond is where I first got the knack.

Jim, who worked as a carpenter when not in college, learned that the local developer planned to fill in the little pond. They wanted to extend our road on a curving route right over my pond. My safari creatures were going to lose their homes and likely lose their lives. I hated it. Here, my brother showed great compassion. He knew of another pond about half a mile away and suggested that we could try to rescue as many tadpoles as possible and walk them down to the other pond. He suggested it and said we could do it together.

The next Saturday, we took all the buckets in the house and started walking loops back and forth between the ponds. We hauled hundreds, maybe thousands, of tadpoles to safety. Jim and I lugged the heavy water-filled buckets, tadpoles squirming in the soup, down the road again and again. We did this all morning long. Even as a youngster, I knew this tadpole transfer was a big deal. It spoke of reverence for nature, appreciation of a special place, kindness and love between brothers, and effort toward something good. I still smile, thinking of those few magical hours.

Another story comes to mind. When I was young, my brother Tom took me on an adventure to Colt State Park in Bristol, Rhode Island. We loved this park. My mom, dad, and I went there several times each year. It had winding roads and trails and a rocky edge on Narragansett Bay. We threw stones and walked among the boulders there. Sometimes, on wintry days, we would park the car and gaze out at the waves.

One summer day, Tom asked me whether I wanted to spend the afternoon at the park. Heck yes. Together, we went in search of nature. He and I prowled along the coves and streams of the bay and gathered little crabs and shells. We got messy and had a super time searching among the reeds and tidal areas. His curiosity about the natural world was clear and infectious. My adventure with Tom that day was a standout experience, but a rare one, because Tom was seventeen years older than I was and away at college for most of my youthful years.

As a teenager, I learned that my two brothers had hiked up Mount Marcy when they were about my age. Mount Marcy is the highest peak in New York and is the centerpiece of the Adirondack High Peaks region. This sounded so cool, so I asked Jim about it. He gave it a thumbs-up, so I asked Dad to see whether we could hike it together. He liked the idea too, so we planned it for the upcoming summer. We trained to get in shape for what we knew would be a hard hike. In the weeks before the trip, we loaded up knap-sacks with rocks and walked tens of miles around our hometown to toughen up our legs.

We did it. We hiked up and over Marcy on an over-night trip. This was my first backpacking trip, the first of my five trips up Marcy over the next few decades. Dad was sixty-four, and I was only seventeen. We hiked in from Adirondack Loj (ADK Loj) via the Van Hoevenberg blue trail and out via the yellow Lake Colden to Avalanche Lake trail. This Marcy hike sure challenged us. The boulders and elevation change were nearly more than we bargained for, but we made it. We loved the rugged summit, the stun-ning views, and the rewards for our efforts together in partnership.

Our guidebook from the 1960s showed a campsite at Lake Tear of the Clouds, just off the shoulder of Mount Marcy, and we planned to spend the night there. On our way up the mountain, we met a ranger who saw our old guidebook, looked at us and our old gear, and probably said a brief prayer for us. He told us our camping plan wouldn't work. The park agency had prohibited camping above four thousand feet and had removed this campsite. Our only choice was to go over the mountaintop and continue down to Feldspar Brook.

Do you know that feeling when you think you are getting close to the end of something, then find out you have a lot farther to go? We felt that way that summer afternoon. We toughed it out pretty well and scrambled our way down Marcy's steep western slope. As we made our way, the trickle of water beside us became a mountain stream. Then a second stream merged with the first. Exhausted, we set up camp for the night where those two streams, Feldspar Brook and Opalescent River, came together. We carried a small but heavy canvas tarp Dad fashioned into a tent with short stakes and ropes. That warm July night, the bright shining moon gave the rocks, trees, and water a soft, grayish glow. It never got so dark that we couldn't see. I dozed but could not get the two rushing, ringing streams out of my ears. Now, so many years later, I can remember the sound of these two streams merging and the gurgling, ringing sound of water pouring over those rocks. That night spent near those streams with my dad was wonderful.

The next day, we hiked out via Avalanche Lake and Lake Colden. Anyone who has hiked in that area knows the scenery is gorgeous, but the hike is a stiff challenge. We made it to Marcy Dam by late morning. There, Dad, exhausted, stretched out on the wooden dam, and I took his pack and mine and headed toward ADK Loj. The game plan was that I would head out to the car, drop the packs, get waters and sodas, return to meet him, and we would walk out together. The plan worked, but not without a hitch. I locked the keys in the car. Yes, I really did this. Tired and nervous about what I had done, I scrambled around and asked the clerks at ADK Loj for a coat hanger. They gave me knowing looks, little smiles, and fortunately, a coat hanger too. I ran back to the car, slid the hanger in between the glass and the rubber window seal, unlocked the door, and headed back up the trail to my dad. Back then, this was a doable trick. I don't know what I would do now in the age of key fobs and electric locks.

Funny, my success unlocking the car door may have been as much of an accomplishment as the hike! Eventually, I met up with Dad, gave him refreshments, and we walked out together. This hike is one of my happiest mountain memories. Locking the keys in the car was not that sort of memory, but the rest was fantastic.

These stories show how I experienced nature in my early years. The time I spent in these special places, with special people, made nature personal. These experiences filled me with appreciation and reverence for nature and the outdoors. Out in these scenes, I felt great serenity—plus, occasionally, nervous energy—when the high rock edges seemed to pull me, or the waters raged. In these places, I felt the urge to be as quiet as in church and take it all in. I enjoyed looking at the vast sweeping views from the mountains and taking in the close-up scenes near the water. I connected to these natural environments and love to see myself as made of that same stuff, that amazing naturalness.

During those teenage years, I read James Fenimore Cooper's *The Deerslayer*. I loved this book, and it has been an enormous influence on my life. He marked each chapter with an opening quotation. Near the beginning of the book, there is a quotation that made me catch my breath when I first read it. It summed up my feelings about the natural world.

Childe Harold's Pilgrimage
[There is a pleasure in the pathless woods]

There is a pleasure in the pathless woods,
There is a rapture on the lonely shore,
There is society where none intrudes,
By the deep Sea, and music in its roar:
I love not Man the less, but Nature more,
From these our interviews, in which I steal
From all I may be, or have been before,
To mingle with the universe, and feel
What I can ne'er express, yet
cannot all conceal.

(George Gordon Byron, 1788–1824)

I hugely appreciated the natural world in all aspects— its woods, waters, and trees—but I also appreciated how the natural world worked in a larger sense. When I say natural, as in natural, not supernatural, my meaning is broader than just the outdoors. As a child, I loved learning about the natural world. I was a fan of science, biology, chemistry, and astronomy. All these subjects interested me as a youth. We had the How and Why Wonder Books in our house, and I devoured them. I knew many tree species and could distinguish them by studying their leaves and bark. I could talk about early rocketry and rattle off the planets in order. I was the boy with the telescope, microscope, Erector set, and chemistry set. Never fully sure how to get the most from these instruments, I still enjoyed them.

Outdoors, I saw the amazing workings of nature. Indoors, I studied how it all worked. I wanted to understand it. The natural world ran in certain predictable ways. Humans could gain knowledge of it bit by bit. This felt right. It was important that I give the natural world the full stage. I saw no need to sell the natural world short, to discount the nature around us for the possibility of a supernatural. Conversely, a Universe executively managed and manipulated by a supernatural being would be inaccessible and unknowable. A supernatural force that oversaw day-to-day life and directed it as it wished was an uncomfortable idea. One could believe it by faith, but never understand it or fully know it. No, I didn't like it. The natural world felt more honest. The appeal of a knowable natural world, a natural world I could play in and experience myself, further widened that crack in my faith.

PHILOSOPHY CLASSES

Exposure to ideas and critical thinking at Siena College was the third factor for my writing those notebook words. I loved my time there. As an accounting major in a bachelor of business administration (BBA) degree program, our curriculum required that we take a full slate of liberal arts classes, and we had lots of electives to choose from. I took more than my share of

philosophy classes because they were so thought pro-
voking. These classes opened doors to a fresh world
of ideas and perspectives. Because of these classes, I
became more thoughtful and a bit more courageous,
as well as a better critical thinker. The philosophy
classes were among the best parts of my academic college experience.

Dr. John Burkey taught my first-ever philosophy
course, and he made a wonderful impression. He did
not advocate any philosophical positions. He encouraged us to think clearly and critically and to express
those thoughts effectively on paper and in class conversations. I so enjoyed these classes. Over my term
at Siena, I took five philosophy classes with him. My
roommate Mike joined me for many of them. We
both loved these classes. Isabel, Mike's girlfriend,
said we both took classes in "Burkeyism" rather than
philosophy. Ha! It wasn't like that, though. He challenged us to think, to learn the material he presented,
but also to analyze and exchange ideas with him and
others in the class.

Occasionally, Mike and I continued our philosophy
discussions back in the dorm room. We discussed
the views of two seventeenth-century philosophers,
Spinoza and Leibniz. We debated the merits of their
respective systems. Mike liked Leibniz, who believed
that the world we see is the best of all possible worlds.
He had a way of explaining how there could be terrible things in the world while still offering a view that
aligned with the church's teachings. This world was

the best it could possibly be. Intriguing, but I liked Spinoza more. He proposed a different way of seeing God, one that differed completely from that of my religious youth. He wrote that everything that exists is God. This appealed to me. He wrote his points in a hard-to-follow geometrical proof style, but I loved the parts I could understand. He wrote that God and the Universe were the same. Wow! It is hard to know what that phrase means exactly, but it is definitely different from the God of my youth. I think there is a connection to those "everything is natural" words from my notebook. His views on God were part of the course that ended before I pushed that handle and stepped out onto the entryway.

Our classes covered system-builder philosophers who tried to produce cohesive views of existence and describe our place in it. They proposed views covering metaphysics, including God, on to views of ethics that fit logically with their frameworks. Oh, this was great. I liked the idea of a grand comprehensive solution. Besides Spinoza, I admired Descartes's approach. He began by doubting everything and searched for one thing to call certain. From there, he tried to add logical elements. I liked his honest and rigorous approach. Because of the examples these philosophers set, I began to think that maybe I could think through these topics on my own.

I remember one time Mom and Dad picked me up at Siena to take me home for a long weekend or spring break. After the first twenty minutes of my running on with catch-up-type topics, I talked about what I learned in my philosophy classes, about René Descartes. Descartes's philosophy was clear and fresh in my mind, so, with a knowledgeable voice, I went through the key points step-by-step. I confidently explained the elements. Dad enjoyed philosophy, too. He took accounting and philosophy classes at Siena forty years before me. He followed along with every word I said and told me I explained them in a clear and orderly fashion. I hadn't done that much in my earlier teen years. He appreciated the logical aspects I spoke about and how I linked the key points. I was proud. Those philosophy classes and the writings of Spinoza and Descartes inspired me. My philosophy classes blew that crack in my faith wide open.

* * *

I was not angry with the church when I started writing, but I was not fully content either. I was willing to consider other ideas. Because of my fortunate experiences outdoors growing up, those ideas tended toward the natural world. Exposure to critical thinking and philosophy was the last piece needed to move me to action. These grand thinkers and their ideas empowered me, helped me feel as if I could think for myself. These three forces came together after class that day. With no warning and no expectations, I put pen to paper in that notebook and out came that critique of what we call supernatural.

As a child, I accepted what my parents and loved ones gave me about faith and beliefs. As a young adult, early in my years at Siena, I became more honest about the issues I had with my faith. I liked the church, but I had some problems with the church's teachings that I could not brush aside. This made me wonder, fostered curiosity, and nudged me to think for myself. That afternoon, I made my first tentative step toward forming my own views. Inspiration came from nature and my recent philosophy classes. This had to happen. It was unstoppable, an opportunity for growth I could not refuse.

Along that walk after class that beautiful spring day, and back in the dorm room, my ideas coalesced into words. Wondering, then writing in that journal, was important and started a habit or practice of thinking and writing about philosophy. I did not journal every day on these topics, but I often wondered about how the Universe worked and about our purpose in life. Over the years, these ideas built up. Then, occasionally, I let them overflow into notebooks or small essays.

Philosophy did not become my career path. I stayed with accounting and since graduating from Siena have worked for over thirty years in management accounting. Though not my career, philosophy, which so captured my imagination back at Siena, has been a lifelong interest. It was more than a casual hobby or curiosity. I focused intensely on these questions and struggled mightily as I tried to make sense of life, see my place in the Universe, and figure out how to be a good person. This has been both a joyous and frustrating pursuit. Joyous because at times I feel as though I made some headway, frustrating because those times were so rare. Answers to these questions are so elusive.

For decades, I have wondered about this amazing Universe and have considered the foundations for ethics and how to live our lives. Now, I am sharing my lifelong relationship with these questions. This *Natural Wonders* essay shows how I wrestled with these ideas throughout my life. Here are my wonderings, doubts, and conclusions about the Universe and God. Here are my views on how to form solid beliefs, how to act ethically, and how to see oneself as an individual but also as a part of the Universe. I share my insights and struggles and provide context by weaving in stories that contributed to these ideas and to who I am today. This blend of wondering, thinking, and experiencing has formed my philosophy and outlook on life.

2

STUCK

That insight after class that afternoon was tremendous and exhilarating but caused me so much trouble. It is hard to unsee something, and it is equally hard to unthink something. That natural and supernatural entry did not come with an undo button. That step onto campus and the short essay that followed changed something in me, and I could not go back. The problem was, I could not go forward either. That short essay was incompatible with my Catholic Church–centric homelife. It was at odds with the views of my family and parents, our rituals, and how we lived. God, spirits, heaven, hell— all were part of my world growing up. Did I mean to deny the existence of the supernatural? Was I a sinner for thinking these new thoughts? Should I cross my fingers? Should I go to confession? The new questioning approach was exciting, but the ideas that emerged were radical. These ideas called me out. They dared me to ask myself who I really was and wanted to be.

What did I genuinely believe? Did I really want to run with these new ideas? I wavered. I couldn't do it. I kept it all to myself, particularly where it mattered, at home, with my family. I stalled, unwilling to embrace my ideas and let the consequences be what they would be.

The natural and supernatural idea was appealing but unsettling. A shiny, sharp object to handle carefully. Even the little notebook was contraband. I wouldn't leave it on the coffee table or talk about it. In that notebook, I wrote words I would not say aloud, particularly in my home environment. I made a statement, then concealed it like a tattoo hidden under long sleeves. I was a blend of bravado and fear, independence, and passive compliance.

If the supernatural and natural question were only an intellectual one, I would have discussed it more openly. I was opinionated as a teen. I argued about sports and politics. This big supernatural question was more substantial and riskier. These ideas could upend my world. They could strain or damage my relationships with my folks. Did I want to risk that?

Adding to the trouble was that I still liked the church and wanted to belong. I relished the comfortable Catholic routines and rituals. I liked the liturgy, the homily or sermon, the music and time devoted to the bigger ideals. My internal conflict was ten out of ten. Sadly, I never once mentioned my struggle or discussed these ideas with my parents. Weakly, I held the conflict inside.

In college, I was alive with innovative ideas, but when I went home, I pretended nothing was going on in my mind. My beliefs were not eroding around me. Everything was the way it had always been, even though that is not how life works. Things change, we grow; but I pretended that wasn't the case. There was a role for me to play, and I played it. I knew what being a good Catholic looked like, and I acted it out. It was an easy habit, a comfortable existence, except it was not comfortable at all. My life then was a tale of two Bobs, neither one a full, honest reflection of myself.

CATHOLIC HOMELIFE

To give you a better feel for why I froze and the depth of my conflict, let me tell you more about my homelife, beginning with my parents, Alice Bradley and Clarence Wilhelm. They were the largest influences in my life. Dad was born in 1920 in Schenectady, New York, and Mom in 1922 in Weehawken, New Jersey. Both had trying experiences growing up in the early part of the 1900s. Dad and his parents lived in a tent village during the Depression, and he served for two years on a minesweeper in the Mediterranean in World War II. Mom's dad died when she was young, and her mom and her sisters moved to Schenectady. Mom and Dad met at a Catholic Youth event before the war. They married in 1945, right after he returned from service.

Mom occasionally told a story that illustrated her faith and her concern for Dad while he was at sea.

She sometimes told this as an add-in to Dad's story of his ship's role in the invasion of Sicily. It goes like this. Mom woke up at night from a vivid nightmare of nothing but terrible crashing waves, high winds, and black, stormy skies. She woke her mother, who was sleeping next to her, who told her to pray. Mom prayed for the waves to calm, for Dad's safety, and for the men on ships at sea that night. She went back to bed, feeling sure Clarence would be safe and everything would be all right. It turns out the seas calmed in a stunning quick turn that night. History books confirm it. This story brought us all smiles of wonder and gave us something big to think about during our holiday dinner conversations. For Mom, this was undoubtedly a miracle.

Mom and Dad had three children in the 1950s, Tom, James, and Evelyn. Then there was a long pause. I was born in 1967. I came along in the Summer of Love, a shy boy in a family of parents in their mid-forties and my three siblings, all in their teens. The 1960s and 1970s were a culturally turbulent time with hippies and old-school parents clashing, war and politics raging. This period was so different from the era in which my parents grew up. I saw what was happening in the world and noticed the stresses weighing on our family. I made it my goal not to be a problem for them. My parents were older and had their hands full. I respected them so much and did not want to cause any trouble. They did not need headaches from me, so I tried not to make waves. This tendency of mine established a pattern that made it hard for me to discuss my religious doubts and emerging philosophy later in life.

We lived in the growing town of Seekonk, Massachusetts. Dad had a good job as an accountant with a plastics manufacturer. Mom occasionally worked outside the house to help raise some money for us. She worked for a brief time in a factory and also as a hotel housekeeper and a census taker. The major challenge for my mom and dad was paying for the Catholic university educations for all their kids. Somehow, they did it. Tom went to Notre Dame, Jim to Villanova, Evelyn to Boston College, and I to Siena. My parents achieved this by being thrifty and not splurging, but we never went without the essentials, and there was always love in our home.

Catholicism was a constant influence in our lives. We always attended weekend service. We received all the sacraments, went to confession, observed religious days, sacrificed for Lent. All of it. We were educated almost entirely in Catholic schools. This was who we were, and I liked it.

At home, we never discussed how we imagined God. We almost never said God aloud, out of respect and maybe some fear. God was a given, and we better be good. God was all seeing, all knowing, benevolent, and loving, but he could be destructive and vengeful, too. As I grew into an older child, then a young adult, the caricature of God developed into more of a general presence and power, but still a being, a force.

God acted in our lives and controlled our potential for salvation in the afterlife. He knew everything we were doing or thinking. We lived at God's will and mercy.

We believed in the devil, too. Mom referred to the devil as "the old boy." The devil was the opposite of God, devious and evil. Sin was the pathway to the devil, and we were on the lookout to avoid it. The devil schemed to take our souls, and we had to be on guard.

Prayer was our two-way radio to connect to this supernatural realm. My mom, particularly, prayed so much. She recited formal prayers but also simply spoke prayers of petition and thanks. I remember her splashing holy water around the house and calling out a steady stream of prayers during strong thunderstorms. We prayed to Saint Raphael when we were traveling and to Saint Anthony when we lost something. A phrase my mom used rarely, but meaningfully, was "pains of mortal sin." She used this phrase only in serious situations. "I forbid it under the pains of mortal sin." That got my attention.

Movies then were heavy with the supernatural. *The Exorcist* and *Poltergeist* scared me so much I could hardly watch them. The spirit world existed in the ether somehow, but it sure existed. God, Jesus, and the Holy Spirit (the Holy Trinity)—these were bedrock words in our family and were as true as true could be. Miracles were real to us. Once, when I had a broken ankle, we drove to the Sainte-Anne-de-

Beaupré shrine in Quebec. I don't think they brought me there specifically for a miracle healing, but I bet they figured it couldn't hurt, and my ankle healed just fine. We marveled at the crutches, walkers, and wheelchairs fastened to the wall by the church entrance, discarded by their owners after their miracles.

At one point, around fourth grade, I came home from school and told my mom I might be a priest when I grew up. Yes, I wanted to be a priest, an interpreter, a communicator, a specialist working in this supernatural realm. For a brief time, I thought I might grow up to be one of these Catholic ambassadors. The priests I knew seemed mature, confident, and compassionate. They were conducting God's works, following in Jesus's footsteps in an admirable version of adulthood. This was the only time I ever thought seriously about the priesthood. I never pursued it, and my mom never encouraged me to head that way. I just needed to let her know I was thinking about it.

Dad loved Christmas, and I joined right in with him. I loved the general magic of the Christmas holiday time. When Mom mentioned an Advent wreath, he made one out of plywood cut into a ring. We had our homemade nativity scene with the little figurines. This was the first decoration we set up each holiday season. Selecting, cutting, and setting up the Christmas tree, always a real tree, was a special ritual for us. Then there were the Christmas carols. Some were beautiful and touching, some upbeat. I knew the words and could play them, rather poorly, on our piano. Christmas was also family time. Dad took time off from work and my brothers and sister, who were away at college, came home. Dad read the nativity passage from the Bible each year on Christmas Eve. It sounds cliché, but we had music, laughter, food, peace, and joy. It was a sweet season.

One year, when I was an older boy but still in grade school, a pattern of light, probably from Christmas lights at a nearby house, formed an image on my bedroom ceiling near the window. This light pattern looked like an angel praying with a halo and clasped hands. This image showed on the ceiling each night around Christmas, and it made me feel special, like a spirit or something had visited me. The image overhead added to the Christmastime magic. I wish I took a picture of it! The next year, the light pattern did not show up, and I missed it. Had I made it go away somehow? Was it something I did?

CHURCH

As a young teenager, I took part in a big event at our church. The parish pastor chose me to be one of the altar boys to lead the procession for the relocation of Our Lady of Mount Carmel from the old church hall to the beautiful new church up the road. For a brief period, Our Lady of Mount Carmel parish included three churches. First there was the tiny but beautiful parish chapel. It was a pleasant little wooden church. It had a high arched ceiling and a pure and peaceful vibe inside. Silhouettes of Mary and the saints adorned the stained glass windows. The pews were gently worn, and a soft aroma of incense hung in the air.

My sister Evelyn was married at this chapel in 1976. She knew the organist, and I remember the music filling the small room. This was our church when I was little. Mom genuinely loved this chapel, and she would go there for daily Mass all week. She seemed to be in her most peaceful state of mind inside this church. When she prayed, she connected to something bigger than herself. I took all this in. We moved from window scene to window scene around the church as we prayed the stations of the cross in that chapel.

Our town grew fast, and the diocese leaders realized the chapel would not work for the booming area so they opened a second church. This church was a large cinder block–style rectangle space with an airy feeling and metal folding chairs rather than pews. It was a practical building, more functional than beautiful, with clear windows rather than stained glass. Both churches operated concurrently, but this church was for Mass on Saturday and Sunday, while the old chapel was mostly for weekday Mass and the occasional ceremony.

This place became our main church and was where we mostly went for Mass each weekend. Roughly every six months, my father would take us somewhere else for Mass, to a different church, one not part of Our Lady of Mount Carmel parish. This was in downtown Providence, Rhode Island. I wish I could remember the name. The place was old school. If you had your eyes closed, your nose could tell you were in church. There was a sweet smell, a mix of candle smoke from the rack of votive prayer candles, a faint feeling of older people in the room. Incense, not from today but from earlier ceremonies, gently sweetened the air. It was quiet, with only soft shuffles and echoed rustling to be heard. Eyes opened to a small, softly lit space made of stone and mortar with a warm but reverent and worshipful feeling. This church clung to the old ways and only tolerated the modern church of the seventies. I'm sure the priest once presided in Latin here. Dad loved it. This environment is where his religious devotion was most comfortable. He would close his eyes and, I assume, find the same connection to something bigger that my mom found in the old chapel.

One summer after the church moved to the hall, I signed up to be an altar boy. I did this in part because my brothers Tom and Jim were altar boys when they were young. Dad told me stories of how they were altar boys for services at Fish Creek, at the outdoor amphitheater there. I wanted to be like them.

An experienced altar boy showed me what to do, and his skill impressed me. He was twelve, but seemed much older, like a pro. The duties are basic, but I was nervous my first time on the job. Besides walking in carrying a lit candle on a staff, there were three major tasks to carry out:

1) Know when to ring the bell. Actually, ring it twice. No one cues you directly; you need to know.
2) Hold the oversized Bible high to make it readable for the priest. You also have to find and flip the right ribbon to open it to the right page.
3) The most important part: preparing for the sacrament of the Eucharist, washing the priest's fingers, and the offering of wine and water.

Carrying out a scripted performance was not my strong suit. I still don't like to line dance. Luckily, my first service was the less crowded, more casual Saturday 4:00 p.m. Mass. I remember it was a sunny summer afternoon. The ushers had cranked open the church windows. The fans turned gently, and the congregation was light, which meant fewer witnesses. Well, I did it. I remembered when to do each part and performed OK. No major hiccups. I enjoyed the good feeling when it worked out. My dad, of course, paid as much attention to my performance as he did to the ceremony. I knew he silently cheered me on from his seat. After church, we debriefed with a little play-by-play review.

After doing my altar boy job for several years, I became one of the more senior members of the team. It became a simple routine to serve a Mass. That was when I helped lead the procession from this church hall to the lovely brand-new church up the road. I felt honored as we walked in a solemn parade, transporting the Eucharist in its tabernacle, about a third of a mile up Route 44.

From 1970 through the end of my high school years, these various churches colored and informed my life. In these churches, I received my First Communion and Confirmation. Here, I enjoyed my sister's wedding, spent time with the youth ministry group, and grew to be a teen. These buildings, with the interior art, mystery, majesty, and community, provided space to think, to contemplate, to ruminate on my actions good and bad. Here, I received my first education on the ideas of God, love, and sin. My church experiences included love and reverence, family togetherness, rituals, and respect. I loved that our family dedicated time each week in a contemplative environment that celebrated and revered something bigger than us, something we deeply honored.

INTERNAL CONFLICT

My parents never made me go to Mass. It was an unspoken expectation. It was simply a matter-of-fact thing. Of course, you went to church. They did not need to say a word. I went along with it, but occasionally I was sneaky. Once, when I visited home from college, I faked it. I made it look as though I went to church but did not actually go. One Sunday morning, home from college for the weekend, I drove myself to the church. Mom and Dad must have gone to the Saturday service. I parked in the church lot, but I didn't open the car door. Mass was about to start, but I stayed motionless in my seat. I stayed in the little Chevy Chevette. I couldn't bring myself to attend the service. For the full hour, I sat in that little car. Every five minutes, I thought about going inside. Mass often inspired me. The sermon and readings often registered with me and made me think. I appreciated the beauty and peace of the place, the time for introspection, and the music. It was that darned theology I struggled with, the focus and devotion to the supernatural. After a while sitting there, still feeling an odd blend of boldness and weakness, I noticed a stirring from the church. Faintly I heard the recessional music, so I started the car and headed home.

Away from my family, in the school environment, I was more open, occasionally outspoken, as I tested my voice on these new ideas. My roommate said, or I read into it, that I was trying to have it both ways. I was a hypocrite because I could not jump all in and embrace my new views. I also could not stop thinking about these ideas. In the end, I said, "OK, fine. I'm a hypocrite." Not ideal, but better than the two alternatives: one, the hard-core break—hurt my parents flagrantly and own these new opinions openly, or two—turn away from this energizing approach to new philosophical ideas. Both options were unappealing. I felt like a traitor whichever way I went. When I joined in with the church rituals, I betrayed my emerging self. When I thought hard about my ideas, wrote some words in the notebook, I felt as if I turned my back on my family and the world in which I belonged. I balked, conflicted. The middle way was the one I picked. I undermined myself for what I perceived would be a kindness to others, maybe also to keep the comfort of my existing life.

Looking back at this, I'm embarrassed and disappointed that I never spoke to my parents about my doubts. I missed an opportunity to share my ideas and connect with them. I think I could have done it gently and respectfully, but I remained silent. Instead of starting a respectful conversation, I kept it all to myself. By avoiding a conversation, I disrespected them and our relationship. By not talking with them, I also disrespected myself. Weak and afraid, I chose a lousy path around the whole topic. I wish I had explored these ideas calmly and gently with my family when I had the chance.

My internal conflict over these ideas lasted a long time. There is no expiration date for this internal conflict. It lingers unless you do something about it, which I did not. After Siena, I worked as a cost accountant with International Paper at their paper mill in Ticonderoga, New York. There, I met my fiancée, and we were heading down the path toward marriage. As you can assume, I was naïve and marriage was not the wisest decision, but we did it. A while after we announced the engagement, Dad talked with me one on one. He said, "You know, you need to get married in the church." The word Catholic was unspoken. He said Mom would not come to the wedding if it was not a Catholic-blessed church ceremony, a sacrament. As I look back at it, I am unsure what to think. My mom was devout, but I believe love mattered more to her. I am not sure whether those were her words or his. Then again, I hear the "under pains of mortal sin" phrase in my head, her voice, and well, it could be. I am sure she was worried about my soul.

At that point in my life, I was not a practicing Catholic and had no regular church parish. My soon-to-be wife was not Catholic. She was a blend of Protestant and Quaker. However, my dad's words resonated with me. Mom had to attend, no doubt about it. I remember going to the Roman Catholic Church in the town of Middlebury, Vermont, where we lived, and meeting with a priest there. As a fully accredited Catholic, I walked in feeling confident. I had my "shots," so to speak. I had paid my dues and, in my mind, deserved to be allowed to take part in the church stuff if I wanted to. He set me back on my heels. He started asking me whether I had a personal relationship with Jesus. What? My dad never had a personal relationship with Jesus. We feared God and tried to avoid sin. Wasn't that enough?

I felt strange talking to him. I had known so many priests in my life, and they were all kind and understanding men. This priest was from a different place. More likely I had moved on to a different place, and my relationship with priests and the church had shifted to awkward. The priest gave me the material needed for a Catholic-approved marriage, the courses and guides called Pre-Cana. Ugh. We did the work. I climbed back on board the church bus. Can you imagine how I squelched my emerging ideas doing this?

The wedding was in a nondenominational chapel at Lehigh University. My fiancée had a good friend of the family, a minister, who would lead the service. However, what would I do about the Catholic sacrament blessing part? Could I find a Catholic priest to join in and tag team the service with the minister and be Catholic enough to qualify?

My sister and her husband, Ed, had a longtime friend who was a priest. He had known me since I was young. I asked him whether he would serve at the wedding, and happily, he agreed. He saved the day. He agreed to join with the minister on the altar and be a dual officiant for the wedding. His presence and his blessing would make the marriage OK in the eyes of the church. Again, "Catholic" was unsaid. Mainly, it would make the ceremony OK with my mom.

Clearly, I did not start this marriage by being true to myself. I look back now and wonder why. Was I too weak to talk to my parents about my ideas? Was I ashamed of myself for thinking non-church thoughts? Did I do this to make everyone happy? I must have known that was impossible. Why did I show so little spine? Maybe it was simply that I did not want to hurt my parents. I often chose the way with the least collateral damage, even if those choices left wounds in me. I don't recommend living this way.

Anyway, in the middle of the service, all was going great, then something happened I can't forget. In a move that we did not see in the rehearsal, the Catholic priest raised his right hand in what looked like an ominous salute. He put his right arm up, palm out, head bowed, and prayed. It was as if he intended holy laser beams to shoot out over the congregation from his palm. It stunned me. My bride looked at me with a subtle but real WTF expression. One bridesmaid wiped her nose, then put her arm out too. In ten seconds, the entire congregation stretched out their arms. Imaginary beams shot from their palms. What was happening here? What are you doing? I guess he, then everyone, was trying to send us holy or supporting vibes through the palms, maybe symbolically. This was so weird. I wonder what my parents were thinking. This was not their normal church style.

In retrospect, I am fine with the entire event and have no animosity toward anyone. This Catholic priest has remained an occasional part of my world when I have been around Evelyn, Ed, and their children, Patrick and Meghan. I most recently saw him at Patrick's wedding, and it was great.

There are two points to be made. One, change is hard. It is hard to move on and grow into new ideas. I wanted to develop and express my own beliefs, but I also wanted to show love and respect for my parents. I wanted them to see me as the same person they had always loved, even as I headed into fresh territory intellectually. Two, doing things for others is good, but it is wise to have a conversation to understand the other person's needs. I wish I had gently talked to my mom about my ideas when I had the chance to hear and understand her wishes. I wonder how strongly she felt that my emerging philosophical thoughts were heathen-like. What would she have said if I had asked?

* * *

My Catholic faith was as much about how I saw myself as it was about actual specific religious beliefs. The church was our group. We belonged. We were the church. I had filled my identity with Catholicism. The church gave us context for life. It connected my immediate family and linked us across generations. My brothers and sister, my grandparents, and aunts and uncles all were Catholic. We had a common point of reference for life. We spoke the same language. Beyond that, the church is global. When you travel, you know there will be a Catholic church available for you with a familiar feel and similar service. When I began asking questions and thinking for myself, I put my identity at risk.

As a youth, if someone had asked me whether I decided to be Catholic, I probably would have said yes. One might say I was Catholic by choice because I chose the church in the sacrament of Confirmation. However, I never went through an evaluation or decision process. My decision to choose the church was a biased one. We did not evaluate all the religious approaches available to us and pick the one that fit best. We did not debate whether we should be Catholic or whether another faith might be better. My family had already set my outlook on life, and near the center of that outlook was faith. I was not about to opt out, to turn my back on family, friends, and much of what I knew and loved. I chose the church that Confirmation Day, but it was a loaded, preset choice, not really a choice at all. We were Catholic in the same way my eyes were blue. Even when doubts were growing and cracks were forming, I would not step away from something so central to my identity.

I continued in my conflicted state for so many years. I moved forward and backward regularly because I was stuck between two noncompatible views and my identity was at stake. The concept of the supernatural made no sense, but I also couldn't see where that "everything is natural" idea would lead me. Unsure whether I could believe in an "everything is natural" idea fully and accept the consequences of owning that outlook, I held to what was familiar, the church of my youth, while simultaneously longing to run free with my latest ideas.

This was a painful time, but the pain was not searing as from a wound. It was not the burning hurt of a fight. This pain was more like emptiness, a long-lasting ache, a dull misery. I was not honest with myself and my loved ones about my ideas. My failure to be true to myself and share with them wounded me. Stings of doubt and cowardice pricked at my insides. The low-grade, but ever-present, dull pang of knowing I disappointed myself throbbed because I did not deal with my conflict.

There was no breakage day when I said I no longer believed in my Catholic faith. I did not come out of the closet of Catholicism. There was no boom. Discomfort accumulated over time, different ideas appeared, and eventually, the cloak of the church did not fit me anymore. I stopped trying to put it on. My "everything is natural" view increasingly made sense the more I lived with it. Repeatedly, I abandoned my ideas and turned back to the supernatural outlook and the church to make others happy or keep the peace, but I never gave up those words.

For anyone who is experiencing similar conflicted feelings around faith and family, know you are not alone, and you are not a bad person. You will doubt yourself and feel miserable a lot. Growth involves reluctant breakage, fear, and acceptance. Inconsistently, I moved one step forward, followed by one step back. Sometimes weak and sometimes brave. There are no straight lines. Just try not to beat yourself up or forget what initially prompted the ideas. Eventually, when the time is right, those ideas will be back by your side. I now see these key ideas on natural and supernatural as friends who stood by me, though I regularly treated them as strangers and turned my back on them time and time again.

3
INSTILLED VALUES

I lived for a long time with that unresolved conflict between my new ideas and my religious upbringing. You can't call a time-out, get life to stop, pause for a bit while you sort it out. Days and years went by while this undecided, conflicted state ran in the background. Despite a conflicted philosophical outlook, I did not lose my way or basis for morality, my sense of good and bad. Even without firm underlying theological support for a way to live, I lived day to day just fine. It was definitely not ideal, but turns out, it was doable. I didn't need to resolve my internal conflict to function. I didn't need a sensible philosophical outlook that reconciled natural and supernatural with my church-oriented life. My character was established as a child, and this foundational outlook gave me direction and boundaries. The values my parents instilled in me, besides purely religious ones, helped form my character, which drove my daily life.

My homelife differed from most of my friends' in that my parents were almost as old as their grandparents were. When I was eight years old in 1975, in the middle of that turbulent decade, my dad was fifty-five. This rooted our views of morality in a broad, historical time frame. Our home did not reflect the values of the day, or decade. Our home reflected values formed in the days of the Depression and World War II.

The ideals Dad and Mom espoused were self-control, discipline, character. My parents did not strongly encourage us to be ourselves or act freely. There was a right way to be, and we should try to be that. Fortunately, a warmth of family love softened all this focus on character, discipline, and self-control. Love was the most important ideal, particularly for my mom. Maybe Mom and Dad performed a good cop, bad cop routine at home well before that was a thing.

My family instilled values in me that helped carry me along. I was like a stone thrown in the air in the sense that my family set the trajectory of my behavior from early in life. Think of it as my launch angle. Even unsupported, the stone flies on as it was initially tossed. Lacking a cohesive set of sound beliefs underlying my behavior didn't matter much. My family's values had already sent me forward, and I continued on that route.

RUGGED INDIVIDUALIST

Besides unconditional love in our home, the ever-present Catholic Church faith, and the appreciation of nature, there was another theme that figured prominently in our outlook and contributed to my values. This theme was hard work, toughness, and persistence. One had to be strong of character. The virtues of self-reliance and strength became another lens through which I viewed the world and myself. Yes, this was another opportunity to come up short in self-perception, to feel a little less than great.

My parents admired the pioneers of the United States, people who set out to create a life in the wilderness or cross the plains in search of a better life. They admired the courageous and dependable heroes of the past and encouraged us to live up to that ideal. The words that express this are "intrepid" and "brave." Those were the key characteristics of the historical people we admired.

My brothers enjoyed, then handed down to me, a music album called *Johnny Horton Makes History*. This album was full of folksy songs honoring America's founders, patriotic heroes, Civil War battles, even Custer's horse Comanche. I loved this album and played it hundreds of times. The song about Snowshoe Thompson and his strength and fearlessness particularly reached me. The songs about Jim Bridger, Abe Lincoln, the sinking of the Bismarck, and the Civil War songs are ones I can still sing parts of today. This, along with the Catholic Church, was our ethos, our worldview. A person needed to be courageous, honorable, active, and brave, besides all the church teachings such as being selfless and a sinner needing redemption. What an odd stew.

In high school, I did well in French one year and joined the French National Honor Society. I had an advantage because I took French throughout grade school at St. Luke's School in Barrington, Rhode Island, so the achievement was not especially grand. Anyway, I received an award at an induction ceremony in the Bishop Feehan High School auditorium. My parents came to the ceremony and proudly took their seats. I gathered with the other honorees backstage until we marched out as a group.

I was such an awkward teenager, uncomfortable in my skin and uneasy with just about everything. I sat or stood onstage as needed, with a stiffness and a cold, aloof attitude that I look back on and regret. I didn't feel superior to the event or my peers, but I felt out of place, nervous, and at risk. Trying to look cool, I acted detached and standoffish as I accepted the certificate and returned to the recipient line. I guess I was trying to look tough and independent. It would have been fitting for me to stand there squinty eyed, cowboy hat slung low, ready for the draw. I had little life experience and I felt uneasy, which translated to coolness, or more like coldness, toward everyone around me.

Later, in the car, Dad tried to compliment me by saying I looked stoical up there. I did not know what a stoic was, but I assumed it was someone who could weather adversity and be strong. Now I understand the word "stoic" better. Dad had mischaracterized me that day. There was no threat, nothing to lose, no adversity to deal with or accept. I wish I had simply smiled and behaved warmly, but I put on a chilly air. This was not stoical. I appreciate my dad trying to make sense of my demeanor and put a positive light on my cool behavior, but no, it was weak of me. I wonder what my mom thought. Did she look at me and say to herself, Can he just smile a little or look pleased?

I won't know the answer, but not too long after that event, I softened my put-on hard shell. Eventually, I realized the world did not need another full-on introvert. I had something to offer socially, however small, and I might want to assume a more open posture in life and be warmer toward my world. I would never be an extrovert, but since then I have found happiness in taking risks in social situations and voluntarily sharing my heart.

In 1985, the summer after I graduated from high school, Mom and Dad and I set out in our Dodge Caravan on a six-week cross-country road trip to trace the routes of the pioneers. This was not a spur-of-the-moment lark. We studied maps and made routes, and selected the roads we would drive, our rest stops, and stays for each night. We wrote away for brochures from the national parks and noted all the KOA campgrounds across America. Our thorough preparation was half the fun. It took us a year to plan and six weeks to make the journey. We'd camp for a few nights, me in a tent, Mom and Dad in the Caravan, then every several days hit a hotel. Along the way, we visited the most popular national parks and had a family adventure. Following along portions of the trail that Lewis and Clark traversed was the best. We admired the scenery and imagined what it was like 180 years prior.

My parents instilled in me an appreciation of the wild frontier and the tough people who made their way out there. Books we loved, and all read back then, were *Three Against the Wilderness* about a family living in the Canadian wilderness and *From Sea to Shining Sea* about George Rogers Clark and William Clark. As a preteen, I became enamored with the fur trappers of the West. I knew the geography of the Rocky Mountains, its major rivers and passes. I could tell you about John Colter, Jim Bridger, and summer rendezvous. You can tell I was clearly the coolest in my age group. All this orientation toward ruggedness and intrepidness formed a big part of my character. My parents encouraged me to be self-sufficient and independent, and I admire those traits today. Yes, while my philosophical outlook was in disarray, I had these values deep in me to draw upon.

My outlook on much of this has shifted over the years. The pioneers were often brave and rugged, but their westward expansion decimated the lives and way of life of the Native people. You could say I now have a more accurate and complete appreciation for the devastation and injustice that went with some things that I was blind to back then. As for independence, well, no one is fully self-made. Opportunity is not dispersed evenly, and we rely on friends and family for help along the way. Like the religious beliefs of my youth, some things needed to be reconsidered. Time and experience added context and depth to the rugged-individualist ideal, and I now see it in a more accurate, less glorified way.

LOVE AND RIGHT AND WRONG

Besides the values of self-reliance and independence, my parents showed me wonderful examples of love and compassion. When I was around eight and we lived in Seekonk, Massachusetts, my grandma and grandpa (my dad's parents) moved in with us. Grandma's health was declining because of Alzheimer's and the early stages of dementia, and my parents were concerned about the two of them living alone in Schenectady. One incident I remember was when my dad called his folks on the telephone and spoke to my grandmother. After their brief conversation, he asked whether he could talk to Grandpa. She put the phone on the counter, walked away, and the phone stayed on the counter. She never went and found him. Dad knew that was not good, but he and Mom were not sure what to do, how they could best help.

Circumstances worsened. Grandma went downhill pretty rapidly. My parents thought it over and made the hard choice, the loving choice. They moved my grandparents into our home. Grandma moved into our converted dining room, Grandpa up to my sister's old bedroom. To give her privacy, we put vinyl sliding doors on the dining room entranceways. A nurse came by every day to help take care of her. She lived in that dining room, in a regular hospital bed, for over two years.

It was an odd time. I enjoyed having my grandparents around, though watching their health challenges was difficult and maturing. I remember two specific mornings waking to the sound of my grandfather calling out loudly, "Ma! Ma!" as he tried to wake or revive my grandmother. I hunkered in my bedroom when this happened and waited as my parents responded and managed the situation, usually by calling 911.

My friend's parents had a season pass to Horseneck Beach, and they asked my parents whether I could join them there regularly throughout that summer. My parents gratefully agreed, and that is how I spent my summer that year. I played at the beach with my friend and his family while back at home my family was taking care of Grandma.

I tell this story of my grandparents' time in Seekonk to highlight my parents' unconditional love. They were very caring, and this was a lot of work. My grandparents did not want to stay in the Seekonk house. They hoped they could go back up to Schenectady and that Grandpa could take care of Grandma at their home. In fact, after about a year with us, Mom and Dad relented, and we planned to take them both back to Schenectady. We were going to take Grandma and

Grandpa back up to their house and set them up to live the rest of their lives together in their own house, with medical help. I remember Mom coming to pick me up at St. Luke's School in the afternoon, after my morning session, and I thought we would go up to Schenectady, but no, she told me my grandfather had a stroke that morning and was seriously ill from it. I don't believe he ever recovered, and in 1979 he died. I was about twelve by this point. My grandmother's condition continued to worsen, and a little after that, she went into a nursing home.

My mom and dad continued to take great care of her while she was there. Alzheimer's and dementia were rough on her. I don't know whether she recognized us when we visited, but that thought never daunted my father. For about two nights a week, for years, Dad faithfully went over to visit. He often brought ice cream from home in a paper bowl covered with foil and kindly fed it to her. He showed loyalty and deep love and care for his mother. This left such an indelible mark on me I can't fully describe it. Eventually, my grandmother died in 1984.

This brings me to another story, a comparable situation, or parallel. Late in my dad's life, he was suffering from declining health and Parkinson's and dementia. Fortunately, for the prior three years, he lived in a multi-level care facility that offered independent living all the way through nursing care, and at this stage of his health, he had a place in a nursing wing. My brother Jim followed in our father's footsteps and showed fantastic care and kindness to our dad. Jim lived forty-five miles away, and he would go over once or twice per week and take a snack or refreshment, or just himself, and talk with my dad for hours.

I saw something beautiful and inspiring in both situations. It was wonderful to see how each of these sons took care of their aged and ailing parents. These examples reaffirmed in me the conclusion that the way you live matters. Even when I had moved away from the traditional motivators of morality, heaven, hell, and such, I could fully see that certain behaviors were better than others and it mattered which ones we chose.

Another significant event happened that registered with me, the opposite of love this time. Back when Grandma and Grandpa lived with us, they paid a neighbor to be a caretaker for the Schenectady house. He watched over the place, cut the lawn, and had the snow cleared. Well, one day we received a call that someone had thoroughly burglarized the house. Crooks had backed a van across the yard to the back porch and stole everything. The furniture in the house was antique because they had bought it decades prior. There were also unique and old-fashioned tools that had both sentimental value and financial value too. It was a violation, a big one, and a mean one. I don't remember whether there was any insurance recovery or anything, and I do not blame the caretaker, but we were all heartbroken. These sweet people had all their possessions taken from them, and the house they had built together violated. This event was such a shock and a blow to my family. It brought concepts of right and wrong to the forefront. The contrast with the love and kindness of my family's parental care was dramatic.

My family made wonderful examples by caring for their sick and aging loved ones. There were no obvious theological aspects. No church stuff here. It was just loving behavior that was hard and demanding, but my family did it anyway. I learned so much seeing all this and being a part of it. Ethics and love were real.

LOVE AND LOSS

Mom and Dad came to visit before Christmas, in 1995, at our house in Bucksport, Maine. We had just moved in that fall. This was their first trip up. The house was old, one of three similar houses built by a ship captain in the mid-to-late 1800s. It had a grand staircase with a newel post in the house's front parlor. I remember Mom struggling to walk up those stairs. She was seventy-three years old and a persistent smoker. I had a feeling this couldn't continue for long. She wasn't strong. I thought the next five years might be a declining period for her. That following spring, it all changed. She went into the hospital for scheduled heart surgery and did not come out. I was shocked. This could not have happened! When we heard the surgery didn't go well, we all rushed to support her and Dad. My family was all at the hospital, and I remember being stunned. Such a loss. Her death devastated us. I knew she wasn't well, but gosh, only seventy-four. I was twenty-eight.

Mom's death hit Dad extremely hard. His voice nearly disappeared into a weak rasp for days. They were married for over fifty years and had lived in that Seekonk house for twenty-five years, and now he was alone. It was so hard on him. I reached out but could hardly help. I saw pain on the faces of my family members, too. This experience helped me form a phrase that describes a truth of life: love and pain go together. You can't have one without the other, and love is worth it. If you don't invest your heart and put yourself at risk, you won't get the joy and rewards of love. You love someone, and pain will eventually follow. It is certain. It is the price you pay. As much as I hate it, it is a fair price for what you get.

As I reread this, I feel it is not reaching the full level of emotion. It is simply hard to express that moment when my beloved mom died. I can't describe the scene well or reflect on our conversations. Maybe this is my arms-length defense for self-survival. There is another story of love and loss I can describe, and maybe because the nature of this is different, I can access my feelings and remember the scene more fully. Mom would appreciate that the story of loss I am about to tell is of a beloved dog.

When I lived in Maine, I had a rescued border collie named Buddy. Sweet and tightly wound, he was a border collie in nature. Anxiously, he walked in circles, room to room, around our house. Eventually, he showed me one of his more impressive abilities. I took him to a nearby park, and he took off to my right on a half-circle loop about forty yards away. He then crouched, eased down with his nose between his paws, and stared at me. This was so neat. I looked around, hoping someone was watching. Buddy then gently walked, in a crouching way, up toward me. He showed me this trick, and we bonded.

I took this as an opportunity to meet him halfway. I learned about border collie behavior and learned the terms "Away to me" and "Come by," which direct the dogs on counterclockwise or clockwise paths. This dog taught me how to be a solid dad for a border collie, to have the most fun and rewarding experience for us both. We went to the park a lot after that first experience and grew to trust each other and anticipate each other's moves.

One morning I came down to let him out of his crate and, unbelievably, he was dead, simply dead in that box. I froze. He was not sick. I called out and slumped to the floor. In tears, I reached in and stroked his body, his neck, and brow. I can still feel the hairs of his fur on my hand and cheek. I loved this dog, and then the loss hit me. Loss is the other side of the coin. One pays for love with pain.

* * *

The first notebook words I wrote were in 1988, but I didn't use them for years. I was unsure of what I believed and stayed in a stuck state. I put further questioning on hold. Had I taken those ideas as far as I could? I was getting by with the values I absorbed as a kid, the examples of love and kindness, and a deep appreciation for love and loss. I look back today and so appreciate all these memories and experiences. The values, the love I saw in how my family lived, all left positive and permanent marks on me.

I knew that if I pursued developing my own philosophy I would connect it tightly to my experiences, particularly the examples of my loved ones. Maybe this is a shade of the classic difference between rationalist and empiricist. Rationalists rely on reason and empiricists on experience. In my case, experience has supplied real-world examples, unarguable evidence of human choices both good and bad. My approach must be a blend of curiosity about ideas balanced with my rich personal experiences.

4
BELIEFS, IDENTITY, AND FAITH

BELIEFS

Nineteen years as a committed Catholic, then a new idea came into my mind about natural and supernatural, and I opened the door to doubt. How could an idea, even a reasonable and solid idea like "everything is natural," upend my world? I mentioned I had cracks in my faith. Even so, how did this happen? What was it about this idea that made it so powerful, so devastating to my existing faith? The answer is that it was a triple threat: clear, sensible, and fit with my experience. A trinity of sorts. My Catholic Church views did not have these three elements. While parts of the church world fit with my experience, the theology and the supernatural elements seemed contrived. Church teachings were complex, often unclear, and mysterious. Some elements seemed less than fully reasonable. I had built my church-based beliefs on weak foundations.

For years, I wanted to go forward and form beliefs I could truly accept, but I didn't know how. Burned when my Catholic faith disintegrated, I was apprehensive and unsure about how to advance. Concerned I might fall in love with new, exciting but ultimately unhealthy ideas, I was cautious. Maybe I would leap into something else that might also let me down, might fall apart later, too. I needed a rigorous evaluation process if I was going to form a cohesive philosophical outlook and a set of beliefs. I wanted to be sure the beliefs I would eventually accept were clear, made sense, and also were true to me at my core.

In 1999, when I was thirty-two, I tried to build out a philosophy and nail down some of these ideas. By this time, I was a wiser, more mature adult, more confident and stable. I was in a seemingly secure work situation at a paper mill in Maine. My married home-life was seemingly solid, too. Sometimes all you get is "seemingly." With the time being right, I made my second attempt at developing my philosophical ideas. I went through boxes at my house, and I found that old Siena-era notebook. As I looked at the pages, mixed emotions flooded me. So much time had passed. I had planted those natural and supernatural words but never cultivated them. I left those ideas on the page and put the page away. It was away, but not gone or forgotten. I read those words over and over, and my pride increased with each reading. Maybe I could continue down a philosophical path and further develop these ideas. I sat down at a desktop computer, not a notebook this time, and tried to make progress in building more solid and reliable beliefs.

It took a few months, but I ended up making a short essay called *Good Consideration*. This was a twenty-four-page little booklet in which I discussed my ideas in areas of philosophy such as God, the Universe, and morality. The title of the essay is punny, but I like it. The title implied that I gave the topics serious thought, or consideration, and the topics themselves were worthy of the effort, or good, in their own right.

In that essay, I put on paper thoughts I've had over the years on these big topics, and I also tackled the process by which I would build out my beliefs. The first part of the essay is about beliefs and addresses the concerns I had about falling too quickly for shiny, innovative ideas. My Catholic faith let me down, and I wanted to be more careful building up my own beliefs in the future. Below are the opening few paragraphs from *Good Consideration*. These words show my first take on how I wanted to form up my beliefs.

As long as I can remember, I've had an interest in the "big" questions of life. "What is the nature of God?" "How did the Universe begin?" "How should we lead our lives?" I was raised as a Catholic in a Catholic family, so these ideas were pretty common. We went to church every Sunday, prayed regularly, and thought about our relationship with God. As a Catholic, I received the answers to these questions before

I knew what the questions were. Eventually, as I got older, Catholic answers didn't seem to make as much sense as they once did. Quietly, I took a fresh look at the questions themselves to see what I could figure out. I gave these ideas the good consideration they deserved. One day I wrote my thoughts down, and now I see I've created a good-sized essay about these ideas. All I did was simply think about these questions and write what made sense. These are tough questions to answer. I don't know if it is possible to answer them. I know that ignoring these ideas and leaving these questions unexplored seems like a missed opportunity for growth and insight.

The society in which we live is not conducive to honest discussion of these questions. Some people don't want to discuss these ideas because they believe they already know all the answers to these questions and their beliefs are absolutely right. These people are often religious, with deep convictions and deep faith. They may preach, argue, or fight about their views, but they are not interested in wondering about them, thinking them through, or explaining them to others.

Another segment of society also avoids these questions. This group includes people who don't see themselves as religious, so they don't think seriously about these questions. They have given up on these questions all together. They discuss practical matters all the time, but don't think much about fundamental religious or philosophical questions. These people have no philosophical foundation, which may hurt them with issues and decisions in life.

I am looking for a middle-ground position. Like the first group mentioned above, I want to have a sturdy set of beliefs, but I don't want to pretend to know more than I do. I want to think these ideas through and develop my own philosophy that is both sensible and reflective of my own experiences. To start this search on the right track, I will begin with a declaration of what I want my beliefs to be.

I want my beliefs to be...

1) **Personal: these beliefs are supported by my experience.**

   The beliefs I choose will fit with my experience. This is to help ensure I do not place too much emphasis on intellectual or scholarly ideas. I will not be too accepting of the ideas of an outside source. I need to see it for myself to believe it.

2) **Reasonable: these beliefs stand on their own reasonableness.**

   The beliefs I choose will be reasonable and stand up to tests of logic and sensibility. I can't prove my beliefs are true, but I will choose beliefs that make the most sense to me.

3) **Clearly stated: these beliefs are clearly spelled out and defined.**

   The ideas I choose must be clearly stated. I will try to work through vague ideas to define them so I can explain them to others.

4) **Flexible: I will revise these beliefs as I learn and experience more.**

I want a set of beliefs I can count on, but I don't want to feel a need to hang on to previously held beliefs when they no longer make sense or I have gained improved insights in life. I will keep an open mind.

I will believe in an idea because it makes sense. I won't believe something because any authority says it is true. I will actively choose my beliefs and be able to explain why I chose them. I can't say that the ideas I accept are true, only that they make sense and fit with my own experience.

These words are over twenty years old. They have stood the test of time. I like them, but I want to bring them up to date, refresh them. Now I have a three-element approach to building beliefs, but all three are essential. These elements are (1) clearly stated, (2) make sense, and (3) ring true to my personal experience. These three criteria work together like a musical chord—an idea that fits the three criteria, plays all three notes, sounds great. An idea that meets only one or two criteria sounds off.

The first element is clarity. Clarity of expression is essential for understanding. When I explain complex issues in my accounting field, I carefully show the key points and present those points as simply as possible. I try to condense meaning down to the essential elements and describe these elements carefully. To help get the point across, I often repeat the point using different words so the listener can hear it from another angle, all to increase understanding. Vague or unspecific language is mostly useless when one is trying to convey a complex point, and philosophical ideas can sure be complex and hard to grasp. Using a clarity-focused approach works in real life on routine topics. Why not use it for the large, philosophical topics we face?

Along these same lines, if you can't thoroughly describe a belief in common everyday language, how can you say you really believe it? You hardly know what it is. A belief is not so esoteric or ephemeral that it is indescribable. That is a feeling. Feelings are great, but a belief is much more. It takes work to process feelings, thoughts, and ideas into beliefs. Our job is to really work at it. We should articulate ideas thoroughly. We should build them out, develop them, and condense them down to essential elements so we can explain our beliefs simply to others.

Another aspect of this is that if you can explain a concept to others, you understand it well yourself. I remember preparing for my CMA and CPA accounting certification exams, and I found that studying something and being able to explain it to others were different. If I could explain it verbally to others, in easy common terms, I knew I would be fine on the test.

The second element is reasonability. I will challenge my beliefs to be sure they make sense. I don't know what is truly reasonable, but I will think clearly about an idea and see whether it is logical and consistent with other principles. It is hard to know whether an idea really makes sense, but I will try. I will challenge the ideas I propose, see whether they stand up to scrutiny and reasonableness.

The last element is personal fit. To say I believe something, it must fit, or ring true, with my own personal experience. I will ask myself whether there is anything in my life experience that supports or conflicts with the concept. Doing this helps ensure that the beliefs I accept will be genuinely mine and fit with my experience rather than be only intellectually appealing ideas. I could fall into the trap and become enamored with a philosophical idea that, upon further reflection, proves to not be true to me at my heart.

This criterion may be the most difficult of the three. This requires that I reflect on the people I have known, the things I have done, the emotions and takeaways from all that living, and then evaluate concepts in light of those experiences. I want to see whether an idea I am considering aligns with who I am: what I have seen, experienced, cried about, laughed over, seethed at, or shied away from. Here, the idea becomes intimate, as if I ran the concept through the gauntlet of the actual world, my own real world.

Beliefs are best when they snuggle up close to us and reflect—even if it is an indirect reflection—the heart of the individual. The criterion of experience is where the idea gets, or does not get, the "Bob stamp," which shows it rings true and aligns with a genuine life, my life. Here, I tell stories of my real life and weave my philosophy through those stories to ensure there is a wholeness to these beliefs.

Let me explain how these three elements work together. First, an idea comes to mind. Can I describe it clearly and in simple terms? If not, I need to keep working on it. Second, I think about whether it really makes sense. Does this idea seem reasonable? If I'm unsure about this, I should reconsider the clarity and sensibility of the idea. Can I refine this idea further to flesh out what it is and what it isn't? When I have sufficiently spelled it out and concluded it holds up as sensible, then it is time to ask the third question: How does this idea fit with who I am at my heart? There is a risk that an intellectual idea will be so appealing that I could accept it and, in doing so, regret it because it could be a poor fit.

Ideally, a belief is a well-considered personal action about a concept. I've seen enough, thought enough, experienced enough to say I believe X statement is true. Ideally, to believe something is to evaluate an idea and accept it as something you will stand behind.

Believing in something is the same as being in a committed relationship with an idea. You choose *this* one.

Believing is an action we take when our level of understanding is sufficiently high. Some people will declare a belief with minimal actual understanding. Understanding is getting as much information as possible about something from many vantage points and figuring out what is and what isn't true. Understanding something is the outcome of a demanding work process. Our level of understanding can be low or high at any point in time, and we can work to increase our understanding.

Below is a set of words that run from the lowest level of understanding at the bottom to the most understood at the top. As you move up the line, you become increasingly satisfied and eventually reach a high level of understanding. For each level of this hierarchy, there is the question of how we came to this understanding. How do we increase our understanding enough to switch on a belief? The tools to help us increase understanding are clarity, reasonability, and personal experience.

	Our Understanding of Something	How to Increase Our Understanding
Full	Understand	
	Accept	
	Get it	
	Lean toward	
	Feel	
	Suppose	Increase clarity of the idea.
	Suspect	Challenge the reasonability of the idea.
	Maybe	Personally experience it.
	Inkling	
	Consider	
	Open to	
	Wonder	
None	Unknown	

What needs to happen for us to accept that something is true, to believe it? The first is to be exceptionally clear. The clearer, more distinct we make the idea, the more likely we are to increase our understanding of it and be able to make a judgment about it. Another way to increase understanding is to challenge it logically. Does it make sense? Last, can we see it with our own eyes, experience it personally?

Sometimes we may leap up this chart because we hear information from an acknowledged expert in the field, but that is weaker because it requires that we trust the speaker. Some people will grab onto a belief without moving up this understanding spectrum hardly at all. They bypass this hierarchy and accept or believe an idea just by hearing it is divine. Many people will pull the belief switch if they hear the concept is holy, blessed. The faith approach bypasses the hierarchy altogether. We can do better than a faith-based approach to beliefs.

Even when I have settled on a belief, I am not 100 percent certain that I am right. I am not saying, "It is." I am saying, "I believe it is." When I believe something, I don't know for sure whether it is true, only that it meets the criteria I have laid out. It is solid but still pliable. If eventually this belief fails, I will reconsider it and potentially move on from it. I won't be capricious, though. I will not abandon an idea on a whim if I have put good thought into it, clearly expressed it, decided it makes rational sense, and concluded it fits with my experience. Beliefs should be sticky. I want a set of beliefs I can count on, but I don't want to hang on to previously held beliefs when they no longer make sense or I have gained insights in life that point out major flaws in the idea.

Word choices and clarity matter even when we talk about beliefs themselves. The meaning is different if I say, "I do not believe something is true" rather than, "I believe something is not true." The first statement is saying that I refrain from adopting a belief in the truth of something. It is saying it may be true, or it may be false. I am not willing to declare it to be true. No position. For this statement, the speaker is staying in the land of uncertainty. It is a bit of a passive statement, but that is fine. The second statement is saying I believe something is false. As I wrote this essay, I tried to be careful with my phrasing, to reflect my true opinion about a concept and communicate it clearly.

I won't be binary or yes/no with beliefs or force a conclusion, an acceptance, or a rejection of everything. I am OK with remaining open minded and unsure of challenging, complex ideas. There is a certain set of things I will say I believe are true. There is a vast area where I say I don't know, have not concluded what to believe. Then there are those ideas I conclude are false. So, I've determined there are three states: believed to be true, undecided, and believed to be false. I am fine if that undecided area is exceptionally large.

One more comment on beliefs. I mentioned that a belief gets established when you reach a certain level of understanding with an idea. That is overly simplistic. It takes time to absorb a belief into how you see your world and live your life. Beliefs are more like slow-roasted food than they are like microwaved meals. A belief becomes, over time, like a friend or family member, something you can count on. You don't get to that state overnight. As it is important to choose friends wisely, so it is important to be careful when adopting cornerstone beliefs such as philosophical ones.

IDENTITY AND FAITH

My personal conflict all those years stemmed from a desire to keep my Catholic identity while considering other philosophical ideas. I stayed stuck in place because I didn't want to risk how I saw myself. When a belief is essential to your identity, questioning it can be risky. Questioning a belief, looking closely at it, and challenging its veracity can reveal information that is hard to swallow. The belief you held for years could be defective, and this could be very troubling. You could find out you were wrong. It is not just that the belief was flawed, but that *you* were wrong. This can be personal.

That our beliefs wrap themselves around us and merge with our identity is significant. Cracks in our beliefs challenge our identities, and faith comes to the defense. Faith is our identity protector. It is the defender of the belief-identity combo, the force that pushes other ideas away, curtails curiosity, and causes us to keep believing in something, no matter what. Faith is a protector that defends our existing beliefs. It is saying, "I have faith. You can't shake it. I'm not listening."

Faith takes an idea and laminates it or chisels it in stone to make it last. It pushes away curiosity and helps us hold complete trust in something, regardless of conflicting information. High faith supplies stability, comfort, and peace. You feel you know something. Your identity is not at risk. It is a soothing state of mind. For those people on the extreme end of the faith curve, they will hold their belief no matter what. They have fully locked down their beliefs. This group will be extremely reluctant to reconsider their beliefs or even allow a smidge of questioning to occur.

We can also think of faith in a physical way. We can see faith as the weight or mass we assign to a belief. Some beliefs are 100 percent set, unchangeable, stuck in place, heavy to move, like a boulder. Low-faith concepts are light and easily shifted. "I believe it will rain tomorrow" is a low-mass belief, easily moved or changed, of low personal importance. "My wife loves me" is an immobile, high-mass boulder of a belief. It takes an enormous amount of counterevidence to move this. How massive we make a belief depends on how important the belief is to how we view ourselves, our identity. If it is a core belief, close to how we see ourselves, we will protect it with faith, assign it all the mass we can.

There is a happy medium on this. There is a "just right" weight to a belief that keeps it from being blown away but does not permanently anchor it. The midpoint is that we believe it but are open to other possibilities. We are powerful enough to shift it, to explore and evaluate opposing ideas that may be better for us.

I mentioned faith as the protector or defender of our identities. We use faith to keep us safe. I mentioned faith in a physical sense as the weight of a belief, how easy or hard it is to shift. There is a third aspect to faith, and it is troubling. We sometimes see faith as a way to apprehend or directly get knowledge of a religious truth. Faith is a personal way to know something in your heart, something science or experience cannot evaluate or resolve. You just know it. It is as simple as "I know it, I believe it, I believe it through faith." Faith is often what people point to when they say why they believe something religious. They believe it through divine revelation or direct access to a truth. I don't support this approach. We have minds, experiences, and the ability to communicate our thoughts to others. We owe it to one another to build our beliefs more thoroughly and to share the underlying support for our beliefs.

The reason this aspect of faith is troubling is that beliefs can be powerful and dividing. Beliefs create a community of like-minded individuals, an *us*, who share a certain belief. When we create an *us* group, we by default create a *them* group, an outside group that has different beliefs and people we sometimes see as different, possibly a threat. If beliefs lead to *us* and *them* group divisions, we owe it to ourselves and others to be careful, critical, and methodical in deciding on our beliefs. *Us* and *them* divisions over beliefs founded by faith are dangerous. Beliefs obtained or revealed through faith are not reconcilable. Faith-based beliefs become unreconcilable differences and fortify the walls between *us* and *them*.

5
BIG YEARS

RETURN TO THE MOUNTAINS

From 1995 to 2003, I lived in Maine, and as a Maine resident, we could apply for and receive preferred approval for backcountry campsites in Baxter State Park. This was a nice benefit of living there, and I took advantage of it. My brothers and I made several memorable trips to Baxter. First, Jim and I went together in 2000. We hiked on a four-day journey counterclockwise through the park, starting and finishing at the Roaring Brook trailhead. That trip was amazing. We loved the nature and wilderness of Wassataquoik Stream, the stunning mountains, and the close wildlife.

The second year Tom and nephew CJ joined, but I could not get the same reservations, so we tried the northern part of the park and found that Black Cat Mountain was tougher than we were. We tried to hike over that mountain to our camp, but Tom ran out of gas. He had no stamina that day. Four o'clock came, five, six, and still the summit was nowhere in sight. I was angry and took his pack to help keep us moving. Still not much progress, still trudging upslope, I sensed what was about to happen. We crossed the peak in the dark. Time was up. With no choice, we bivouacked for the night near the peak. We spread out sleeping bags in the woods, under and on top of pine branches, and did the best we could. As a punctual and rules-oriented guy, I was worried that when we did not show up at our designated lean-to, a ranger would notice and the *Bangor Daily News* headline would be "Missing Hikers Feared Dead."

What a tough trip! I swore I would never hike with Tom again because I thought he did not take the hiking challenge seriously and didn't prepare or train for the effort. I must not have meant that oath because we hiked Baxter for the next two years: one year with Tom, Jim, and me, and the last year, 2003, with all four of us again. I think I needed those two last trips to get past that hard year. Tom told me that planning and executing that last trip were the best things I ever did. I am proud we didn't give up after that tough first year.

Mountains continued their call. Jim, his friend Charlie, and I went out west and hiked the Absaroka-Beartooth Wilderness. We did this in 2005 and 2006. We searched for Martin Lake, deep in the Beartooth Plateau. The first year, mosquitoes made us insane and drove us to an early exit. The second year was much better. We carried out a grand five-day journey over the most rugged and beautiful country one could hope to experience.

I have written so much about hiking and camping because this is how I most often and deeply experienced nature. While in these natural settings, I experience a reverence for nature and awe in the Universe that we so fortunately get to enjoy. Besides the Universe/God/Nature presence, there are the people who have joined me. I have so enjoyed sharing these experiences with my loved ones. The times with Tom and CJ in Baxter had challenges, but these experiences have matured into glowing fond memories, ones I wish I could repeat. These experiences outdoors reaffirmed my appreciation for the natural world, which had prompted me to begin my journal that afternoon at Siena.

ROUGH YEAR

The twelve months from November 2007 through October 2008 were the hardest ever for me, but by the end of that period, hope was at hand. In November 2007, I drove up to Farmington, Maine, to appear in court for divorce. Fifteen years, four states, four cats, two dogs, multiple jobs, and no children, we ended it. It was an amicable split, and we did not use attorneys. The event in court took only thirty minutes. I remember staying at a hotel in Wilton, Maine, the night before and standing out by the lake, having a few beers, viewing the stars and woods all around and thinking, What has happened to my life? I was forty, my fifteen years of marriage had amounted to nothing, both my parents had passed already, and I was feeling alone and a failure. The marriage was not excellent. We were not great for each other, but I had made a promise, a sincere promise in the presence of my loved ones, and now I was signing papers to end it. I still had my two brothers and sister in my life, so I was not really alone, but I felt like a low-integrity loser.

Then, in 2008, my sister, Evelyn, and brother Tom both died. Can you believe that? About my sister: She was an RN in New Jersey, married with two children. Evelyn found out that she had pancreatic cancer in 2005, and we all cringed. We knew what this meant. For two-and-a-half years she rose to the challenges of the cancer and the treatment. She was wonderful, and I am proud of her. I went out to visit her early in 2008, just a few months before she died. I was low because of my divorce, and she was having it rough at a physical level. We related sweetly to each other, though I don't want to imply that my circumstances were like hers. She had likely fatal cancer. I had post-divorce self-loathing.

I have talked little about my sister in these essays, and that is an omission. What a kind person. We had so many happy Christmas gatherings at her home. She and her husband, Ed, hosted the warmest family gatherings imaginable. There was something unassuming, kind, and peaceful about her I still miss. Evelyn, my closest-in-age sibling, died March 15, 2008.

Tom's death shocked us all. Jim and I were together in late 2008, golfing at the Robert Trent Jones Golf Trail in Alabama. He had just headed back to New Jersey on Monday when our world went off the rails. We heard Tom was in intensive care after a fall down the stairs at his house. He was dying. I could not believe it. He was fifty-eight. Evelyn had a disease widely understood as fatal and lived with it for years. We knew a call about Evelyn would come one day, but Tom's was a different situation. I would not say he was healthy, but he had no cancer-type condition. It was a shock and hard to believe. He died on October 28, 2008.

As I look back at these two deaths in 2008, I find it interesting to note the religious aspects of their situations. Evelyn and Ed appeared to me to be very devout Catholics. I think they really believed the words. He was a principal of a Catholic school, and he and Evelyn were associated with, and were comfortable with, the church. When she died, she was a practicing member of a parish church. That community embraced the family. The church was a vital part of helping the family deal with Evelyn's passing. In Tom's situation, something was different. He and his family were also practicing Catholics, particularly when their children, Katie and CJ, were young, but I get the sense that the church did not have the same draw and community role that it had for Evelyn and Ed. This is not a criticism. Everyone finds their place or comfort level with a church and its teachings, a place somewhere on a continuum. Evelyn and Ed were high on this scale, Tom and Eileen maybe less so, and me close to zero and dropping.

Those two years, 2007 and 2008, were tough. Toward the end of that time, I was mostly back on my feet. I was at a place where I felt the pain of loss, but I also found independence, and I stopped criticizing myself. I dated for the first time in ages, found value in myself. Even as I owned my marriage failure, I realized I was still intact. Life went on. It is funny how your head can swing from a low to a high by accepting your circumstances as they are. At least I experienced this in late 2008. By the end of that year, I was solid in myself again, comfortable and accepting of my flaws, and had found my heart's best friend, Carolyn. Things were looking up!

LOVE AGAIN

Carolyn Rock and I met in late summer 2008, and I knew I wanted her in my life—as a friend, a running partner, or more. Anything, as long as I could spend time with her. Yes, I was falling in love.

On June 12, 2011, on the rooftop of the Madison Hotel in Memphis, we married! We had both told ourselves we would never get married after our first marriages failed. No way! Well, this goes to show you that your opinions can change. My wish to marry Carolyn was because of my deep love for her, and I also wanted to team up with her to help her, her daughters, and me form a happy life together. I wanted to join her three-person team. I did not want to separate her out but to jump in, and jump in, we all did. Shortly after the wedding, we all moved into my house in Collierville. Wow, now I have not only a wife, but daughters!

Becoming a parent was much more challenging than I expected, based on my many years' experience as an uncle. Plus, teenage girls can be a handful. Occasionally, I would be a watchdog, or border collie, protectively watching over the "sheep." I had so much fun, though. I was the geek who expressed joy and wonder on college tours. Oh, the fun and learning that awaited them.

Carolyn and I, as parents together, tried to act with unconditional love in how we treated each other and raised the girls into adulthood. I said from the start that my role was to show great love for Carolyn and to show these girls that they can achieve anything if they try super hard at it. This has been the most rewarding period of my life. Church was not part of it. Nature, conversation, travel, humor, and kindness were the key parts. These have all characterized my life with Carolyn and the girls, our family!

Of course, I wanted to share my love of the Adirondacks with Carolyn, so I brought her on a trip to the region. Carolyn and I hiked Mount Marcy in a single day up the blue trail and cut the yellow along Lake Colden and Avalanche Lake back to ADK Loj. This was quite a feat, and it was darn near impossible for us to walk the next day, but we did it. I shared this magical mountain place with Carolyn, and I could not have been happier or more proud. Seriously, she amazed me. The hike was a tough one. I had never tried this route in one day. No one in my family had. The ranger on top of Marcy looked at us as if we were foolish. Maybe she asked herself whether she'd have to rescue us as dusk fell to night. The ladders by Avalanche were plenty tough, as was the darn trail signage, which seemed to repeat the same distance to ADK Loj no matter how far we walked. Fortunately, I did not lock the keys in the car this time! The pizza back in Lake Placid that night was so tasty and satisfying.

As I reflect on the losses and my new love during this period, I am struck by how significant these few years were. This was a crucible period and somehow, I came out of it on my feet. The breakage of my first marriage tested the ethical views I started at Siena and refined with *Good Consideration*. The values instilled in me when I was young, plus the church teachings, all would have declared me a failure and a sinner. I had to reconcile my emerging views on ethics with what was happening in my life, what I was actually experiencing.

Beyond that, Evelyn's and Tom's deaths confronted me head on. These deaths could have pushed me back toward a church-oriented view that embraced the supernatural and all its trappings. It did not. Longing to reunite with them in heaven and wishing my brother and sister salvation in an afterlife is what many people were saying to me or implying. I didn't get on board that bus. Oh, I missed them and still miss them so much, but I did not reconnect with the church. I wondered about what happens after you die. These thoughts colored my developing philosophy as it relates to our sense of self, mortality, and immortality.

Parenting brought on new responsibilities. This role could also have pushed me toward regular Sunday services and a fresh embrace of Catholicism to set what others might have considered as a good example, but it did not. I was in my forties and could finally be true to myself, at least much more so than as a twenty-year-old.

This period from 2007 to 2011 was crucial. It challenged me to find out who I was in my heart. I occupied my skin in a way I had not before. I let the fear in me subside. The reasons for being stuck that tied me up when I was younger, those issues that prevented me from moving forward with any coherent philosophy, simply eased. I was free, a human, a life on this planet, free to live my life as best I could. So many of the outside-provided boundaries that had directed and tormented me in my past became much less influential. Maybe, at my core, I finally believed I was as good as the trees, grass, or squirrels.

6
AMAZING UNIVERSE

The Universe amazes me. From the intricate working of cells to the enormous forces of physics, it all astounds me. Cellular reproduction, growth and healing, sense perception through hearing, sight, smell. It is all fantastic. Then there is the mental capacity we have for reason, understanding, and communication. I am so awed and impressed, constantly wowed by the seemingly magical ways in which the Universe works. I like to think of myself, and all of us, as parts of this amazing Universe. Every once in a while, circumstances come together to help me see afresh just how wonderful this world is.

Carolyn and I lived in the town of Libertyville, Illinois, a small town north of Chicago, for five years, starting in 2016. We never expected to live in Illinois, but that is how it worked out. My previous company in the Memphis area severed me, and after a few months, I found an opening at a different company in Illinois working for a manager that I had worked for previously and respected very much. The job choice turned out to be good for us. I liked the work, and we liked the town, but the timing of the move was tough. Alex had graduated from college at the University of Tennessee at Chattanooga, UTC, and Sammy was about to start college at Middle Tennessee State University, MTSU. They moved out of our house in Collierville, Tennessee, and we immediately moved nine hours away. That was a trying time for us all.

Libertyville proved to be a good fit for us and while there, I began work on *Natural Wonders*. We often sat on the porch or in the backyard. Carolyn read, and I sometimes wrote. One sunny fall day, Carolyn and I were sitting out back at our house, and everywhere around us were maple tree seeds. Seeds were continually falling and covering the ground. One fell onto my lap. I picked it up and looked closely at it. Have you ever looked closely at one? These are beautiful and so functional. The seed is at one end and emerging from it is a large, veined wing. The wing caught my eye. It is so thin, almost translucent, with an airfoil shape that enables it to spin when it falls from the tree. It floats gently down, covering some distance as it works its way lower.

I looked at this maple wing and asked Carolyn a question. "Do you think this design happened over time, over millions of generations of seeds falling?" Seeds fell and piled up under the tree for ages. Then a mutation happened, and a filament grew out of the seed, which caused odd movements when falling. Then, over more ages, the successful filaments with more breadth and shape became the evolutionary winners. Science proposes this with the theory of evolution. I asked more questions. "Do you think it could be something different, that there is a force built into nature that tends life toward efficiency and beauty more directly? Could there be something in the Universe, in nature, which tends organisms toward betterment? Is intelligence somehow integrated in the Universe?"

We see intelligence as an attribute of an individual, as in "this person or animal is intelligent." Perhaps intelligence is not a feature of us, not something we have. Maybe it is an impersonal attribute or force of the Universe, and we take part in it. We don't own it. We use it. It is not of us so much as we are of it. In this way, is it possible it would not be trial and error, evolutionary survival over generations and over time, but a more active lean toward better function? She did not know the answer to these questions any more than I did. We don't know the answers, but we liked the question. On that sunny afternoon, this alternative idea seemed appealing.

One day on a run with Carolyn, we saw the most beautiful blue bird by the gravel path. This bird was so amazingly blue it was absolutely striking. How does a bird like this exist without the magic of Disney? What path brought this iridescent bird to this place and time? Is this bird the one hundred millionth in its line and, over time, through natural selection, the line became ridiculously fancy and gorgeous? Alternatively, does life, cellular growth, naturally lean toward the most beautiful and most efficient possible such that there is more in play here than natural selection, random trial and error? Maybe intrinsic development toward betterment is in the fabric of nature.

Right then, I realized something. It doesn't matter which view is right. I can accept that the process is a slow evolutionary one that happens over eons through natural selection and trial and error. I also think that maybe there is more. It may lean toward beauty and efficiency as a part of the fundamental ways nature works day to day. Either way, the Universe gets there. Somehow it happens. It works. The Universe intelligently moves toward betterment regardless of the mechanism. The Universe seeks betterment. In one case, through evolution, it is over time, over many, many individual lives. In the second case, as a built-in force or characteristic of nature, it is quicker and ongoing. The outcome is the same, a real tendency toward efficiency. Beauty, order, and efficiency are each a part of the Universe, and that is wonderful!

Recently, Carolyn, Alex, and I toured the aquarium in Chattanooga, Tennessee. It wasn't our first visit, but it had been a while. When Alex attended UTC, she had a membership and we joined her several times. This visit, like most, amazed me. There are two exhibits, two separate buildings. One is called River

Journey and one is called Ocean Journey. We started in the River exhibit. The tour starts at the top of the building and you walk down through a depiction of a mountain forest with small rivulets running that eventually form streams and rivers. The water flows and widens. Floor by floor you see the unique life found at each river stage.

As you walk, you encounter small fish and amphibians in the damp forest environments. Gosh, the turtles alone are something. They seem to be in every color and size. The salamanders reminded me how, as a child, I used to hunt for them under rocks and logs in the forests near my house. The aquarium has frogs, snakes, crayfish, and a wide variety of minnows. Eventually, you get down to larger waters with fish such as perch, trout, and bass, then on to huge river beasts such as carp and sturgeon. The diversity of life in this widening, strengthening river environment fully captivated me.

Our next stop was the Ocean exhibit. The diversity of creatures here blew me away. The ocean has life in every imaginable style, shape, and size. There are all kinds of fish—thin like pencils, fat ones, pointy faces, flat faces, and enormous bellies. Their colors are all over the board. It is amazing. There are seahorses, king crabs, jellyfish, beasts with scales, beasts with skin, exoskeletons, cartilage, you name it. What a menagerie this is. It is just a small sample of the ocean's diversity. This tour reminded me how amazing the life surrounding us is. It is jaw dropping. On this trip, we did not venture to the rooftop area to view the butterfly exhibit, but imagine my awe when we toured it on our previous visit. Those colors, the delicateness and beauty of the butterflies; it was stunning!

I thought more about how life grows. This thought started with imagining a single cell dividing. I wish I knew science, particularly biology, better, but hopefully I can get the idea across. Imagine a cell, then see it divide into two cells. Then see it divide again, on and on. This division is amazing, but there are other cool elements. For instance, somehow this cell clump can find up from down, left from right, head from tail, recognize spatial orientation. Does it have a GPS? Somehow the cells that form the head grow at one end, cells that form the limbs, almost perfectly measured apart, grow at the corners. This is astounding. How can this be? DNA, proteins, chemicals are all involved, but is this the entire story?

Often when I have an idea about life, or wonder how it works, I look at our dog, Bradley. I don't know which is the better example, her ears or eyes. Let's go with ears this time. Her ears are symmetrically placed. Each ear is about four inches long with an equivalent sweeping taper and curve. The physical orientation and symmetry amaze me. Never mind the functionality of the ears in picking up sounds. How can this be? Does the organism keep track of the developing being and map it, or does each part navigate through cellular dead reckoning? Does each cell communicate with other cells to position itself? How are bodily organs and tissues situated so usefully and function so well?

If you did a real-life test and invited one thousand of your closest friends to a field and gave each one a card that specified a portion of a body—ear, eye, nose, paw, heart, liver, et cetera—then blindfolded and gagged each one and let them loose in a big field with the mission to assemble into the shape of a dog, how in the heck would they do it? They couldn't do it. Without a vision of what the full shape needs to be, a spatial orientation recognizable to all, communication, and leadership, they will fail. It will not resemble a dog. How does biological growth happen as wonderfully as it does?

A) It is all programmed in the DNA and plays out like a script or program. I don't think so.

B) God oversees everything and makes all this happen. I have issues with the view of God as a supernatural being directing things.

C) There are attributes in matter (cells, tissues, proteins, molecules—who knows what?) that have the essence of intelligence, organization, efficiency. These natural but astounding attributes orchestrate the growth process. The Universe knows what it is doing.

At first, I thought the best answer was option A, a set routine or script played out or performed naturally, like a program or app running. Maybe this "music" plays the same as it does when a player piano operates. Then I envisioned an inflatable bouncy house, or blow-up Santa decoration. It is packed tight and folded, but when we blow it up with air, the bouncy beast unfolds and expands, taking the designed shape. Could this be what happens when cells grow to become full organisms? I don't think so. It is too simple an answer and does not allow for what happens in a developing life when something does not happen normally. A developing fetus with three limbs, not four, is not a failure. Amazingly, the organism adjusts and grows skin over the area where the gap would be. Instead of a bust and the death of the nascent life, the organism adapts. How can this ad-lib, improvisation, happen? Hard to imagine that flexibility built into a script. The bouncy house or inflatable Santa concept cannot be it.

Option B is what many people would say, but I do not believe in a supernatural director.

Option C is exciting. Are there examples of cellular functions that support a view like this? I don't know. There is healing in organisms. How do organisms know to direct healing efforts, chemicals, cells to a specific location in the body? Are there body map coordinates? There is so much I don't know. I find the idea of a Universe that has built-in intelligence or power of organization extremely appealing.

I remember a little about ancient Stoic philosophy, and they used a word called logos to describe an essential logic or intelligence inherent in the Universe. My ideas on intelligence in the Universe align with this. I found an *Encyclopaedia Britannica* reference online: "logos, (Greek: 'word,' 'reason,' or 'plan') plural logoi, in ancient Greek philosophy and early Christian theology, the divine reason implicit in the cosmos, ordering it and giving it form and meaning." This is what I have in mind. The characteristics of intelligence, order, wisdom, and so forth are right in the fabric of existence. I don't believe in a supernatural God, a chef, planning and crafting this magnificence. Like everything else, order, wisdom, reason, efficiency, and beauty are elements or characteristics of the Universe.

7
INDIVIDUAL AND WHOLE

L ately I have been thinking about our individuality and what our impermanence means. My body will die, that is certain. This scary fact is probably what prompted someone to imagine the idea of heaven. Heaven, an afterlife, is appealing because it neutralizes death. It gives us permanence, eternal life, if we behave or at least repent before it is too late. My view that there is no supernatural means I can't believe in a traditional supernatural heaven. Also, the idea of heaven is unclear, not reasonable, and I have no experience to suggest it exists. What does this say about my outlook on life? Am I a very temporary animal with a finite life span and that is the complete story? Is there any view of immortality that would fit with my metaphysics views?

Well, there might be something. I can imagine a type of immortality, but to do so, I need to think of myself differently. I need to broaden my sense of self to see myself as a piece of the Universe. We can all do this, to think of ourselves more like extensions of an infinite Universe rather than as finite individual beings. If we say we are the Universe, and we really mean it, we are immortal and infinite, like the Universe is. The trick is, can we see ourselves this way? Can we give up our extension, or single self, for the idea of self as an expression of the Universe?

This takes me back to that moment after the philosophy class when I stepped through those doors and felt kindred to everything around me. This way of seeing myself startled me with its simplicity and obviousness. Of course, I was part of what I saw around me. More intimately, I *was* what I saw around me. That seemed obvious then and still rings true.

Look at humans. For all our differences, we are very much alike. There are billions of us. From afar, we look much the same. We are so alike, with similar arms, legs, torsos, smiles. We did not create or design ourselves. Our parents did not design us specifically. We are part of the Universe, extensions of it, splashes, or expressions of it.

Once I started this thought, I ran with it. I imagined an ocean scene, a stormy ocean scene with huge rolling waves. If we zoom in, we can picture a single individual wave in that scene. The wave begins with a slight bump that grows over time to a full-size mature wave that traverses the sea and rolls on toward its end, eventually crashing and dissipating on the shore. The wave existed, thrived, reached its potential, and then ran out onto the beach. This wave has an individual existence. We can describe it, define it, and characterize it individually, but this wave is also part of the whole, the sea. What is the wave? Is it an individual with its own identity, or is it the sea?

It is the same as changing the focus of a lens. Focus in, and you see the wave; broaden out, and you see the ocean. Both individual units and the whole are two views of the same situation. The wave is an individual bump and the ocean.

Several other illustrations occurred to me. The first is pixel dots or mosaic pieces and the full picture that they represent. When we zoom in, we see dots. Zoom out and we see the broad picture with its full meaning. Another is individually typed letters and the full book. Letters are real and essential, but the full meaning is in the whole, the relationship and order of the letters and what they say. Last, individual music notes are the "focus-in" identity, and the chord or melody is the "focus-out" understanding or identity. In each case, there is the individual and also a larger identity of which it is a part.

Taking this to a human viewpoint, I am an individual, but I am also equally everything around me. This may be a hard view to accept. We are comfortable acknowledging the duality of the wave and the sea, the dot and the mosaic, but we rarely see ourselves in this dualistic way.

Can we see ourselves as more than skin-bound individuals? Maybe all lives are not individuals in competition with one another. Could it be that life is one vast organism with many filaments, expressions, or visible touch points? The pushback is that we honestly feel like individuals. We can point to three key attributes that distinguish one individual life from another:

Boundary—each life has an outer edge. This is a place within which the cellular functions are those of the individual life, beyond which lie the external, other lives. It's hard to argue with this. Each life has a separate edge, skin, or barrier between that life and the world outside it.

Autonomy—each life acts mostly on its own behalf for its own good. Lives seem to be self-directed. Regardless of physical boundaries, there is something more separating, and that is the sense of individuality, the sense of individual control and independent direction.

Duration—each life is finite. Individual lives are impermanent.

These are legitimate points that support an individual-only existence, but they are weak. Imagine for a second that you could see all the microscopic life surrounding you. Yes, like one of those ultraviolet lights that reveal unseen uglies on hotel sheets. Imagine seeing every single-celled organism around you. This is kind of horrifying. I prefer to think of this space as empty. Anyway, just imagine it. The floor, particularly, is probably a solid sheet of life between you and the next person over there. The air too may be filled with bacteria or minutiae of life. There is a real density to the fullness of life around us. We are awash in life, and this life pushes against our apparent individual boundaries. This happens through sickness and disease. Viruses and bacteria constantly invade us. Maybe our physical life boundaries are more porous than thought.

Where does my boundary end and the rest of the Universe begin? There is no absolute, firm line. Imagine a blood cell and an arterial wall cell within my body. These are separate and unique. They are different in composition, characteristics, looks, and function. They each have boundaries. But do you know what? These are part of the same life, me. So maybe boundaries, even robust ones, don't separate individual lives. Perhaps physical boundaries are not a good criterion for the view that individual lives are separate.

What about autonomy? How does the example of the blood cell and arterial wall cell illustrate autonomy or the lack of it? It seems as though these cells have a certain level of autonomy, but they still are part of the whole. They are not individual lives, they are parts of the organism's life. Maybe autonomy is not as key a factor as I thought.

How about duration? Each of these cells has a life-span, but that finite aspect does not make each cell an individual life.

This brings to mind the classification of biology, including cells, tissues, organs, systems, organisms. Is there maybe one more step up that chain that puts organisms into the whole? Could each of us be an extension, filament, element, instance, or expression of life? Life is one, not parts that appear to be individuals. This is an interesting idea.

A phrase came to mind: "I am the Universe with a sense of individuality." Can the wave, the mosaic dot, the typed letter, the musical note, and each one of us all mingle our own identities with the full world of which we are a part? We achieve eternal life when our identity merges into the identity of the whole. If you are just the traditional you, the 190-pound cellular blob pictured on your driver's license, your life will be finite. If you *are* the Universe, you live forever. With this outlook, we can see ourselves as immortal. The tight focal point of our identity will die, but the broad view of ourselves as of nature or the Universe continues. Immortality is ours, even as our zoomed-in view of self ends. We are all portions of the eternal Universe. Because of this, we never end.

In the last few pages, I have suggested that we should see ourselves as extensions or expressions of the Universe. I implied we should shift our focus, or blur out our individual identities, to recognize that we are aspects of a larger whole, minimize the individual in favor of the Universe. Well, maybe not so fast. The Universe took specific actions to assemble, congeal itself into a functioning unit. I, this two-legged bag of flesh, am something that the Universe built. The Universe invested biological resources in my skin-bound mass. My individual blob of life matters, and it can positively or negatively affect the whole. The individual blob, or organized unit of the Universe, is the tool, instrument, or hand of the Universe. The individual makes things happen. It is the action part, and it is the part we get to direct and control. You and I are the finite entities or assemblies that are how the Universe gets things done. If I discount the unique-ness of the attributes assembled in this Bob-blob, the responsibility and opportunity presented as this indi-vidual, then I am doing the Universe a disservice. A phrase I like is the following: "I am the Universe with a Bob Wilhelm perspective, and I am also a self-di-rected, independent agent of the Universe." Both perspectives are valid.

There is a useful analogy here. The relationship between a cell and the organism that holds the cell is like our individual relationship to the Universe. The cell is a part of the organism. Cell and organism represent person and Universe. Following the logic of the earlier points, one could think my ideas down-grade the cell because it is an element or extension of the organism, and only the whole matters. Thinking of it now, I say no. The cell matters to the organism.

It is essential to the organism. The cell, every cell, has a crucial role to play.

The view I accept is that you are both an individual self and an element of the entire Universe. There is the "unit you," what we think of as our self. This is what you control. I call it the Bob-blob. This is me as first-person singular, the cells that coordinate together, bounded by skin, to form the person we know. Then there is the "all you," the rest of the Universe you are a part of but do not control. Resources shift constantly from the "all you" to the "unit you." As you live, eat, breathe, and so on, the "all you" provides resources to "unit you." More accurately, the "unit you" takes resources, sometimes violently, from the "all you." These words for "you" are not working well. How about you singular and you plural? No. How about You Finite (F) and You Infinite (I)? Now we are getting there. You (F) and You (I). There are two ways to see yourself, with both being legitimate: individual You (F) and whole, infinite You (I).

Seeing ourselves from these two perspectives is a fundamental change. There is no longer an "other" because You (I) includes all. There is still a specific self, a You (F) that you direct and for which you are responsible. Together, these two views of self create the full picture of us. While this dual view of self is complex, it is very rich.

8

IDEAS OF GOD

I t is hard for me to say the word God. Just discussing it feels daring. The pure power we allow for God makes talking about God seem like a brazen activity. That word is loaded with meaning and has different meanings for different people, but it is an electric, explosive word just about everywhere. I can't let that cause me to shy away. I am trying to develop a coherent philosophy, and this means addressing this idea head-on. Fortunately, the idea of God has always been with me. My concept of God has changed over time, but it was always a part of my life, often in the background, occasionally in the foreground, during my moments of deepest longing and joy. My homelife was full of reverence and respect for a higher power. We prayed to God regularly, not just in church. My family encouraged a sense of wonder and reverence for that divine power. When I wrote those notebook words about natural and supernatural and said there was no supernatural, did that mean I could not believe in God? Did I need to drop the idea of God entirely? Is the idea of God completely incompatible with a non-supernatural outlook?

The most obvious answer, but a hard one to accept, was that I should discard the idea of God. A supernatural God-being with almighty power did not fit with my emerging natural-only view. The more I thought about the idea of a supernatural God, the more uncomfortable it became. I found it almost offensive. I did not want to believe a capricious supernatural being could mess with our world. The problem is, I wouldn't give up fully on the idea of God. In my heart, I felt that in some way, shape, or form, divinity existed. My ideas on natural and supernatural challenged my outlook on the supernatural and God, but I never stopped thinking there was so much to revere in the Universe. Earlier I talked about how ideas need to fit with, and ring true with, life experiences. A zero-divinity world in which we have nothing to be in awe of did not suit me. Do I really want to say there is no God?

Stuck on this key question, I was in a state of limbo again—not conflicted in the same painful way I was before, when church and family issues were palpable, just not sure how to move forward. I kept searching for a way to hold on to my awe and reverence but to drop the supernatural. I tried to craft this idea of God, work it over and over to see whether it could create a view of God that stood up to tests of clarity, reason, and experience.

What to believe about God is one of the most important questions we face, but it is so daunting. It is so hard to form a belief that you can be comfortable with in your head and heart. I thought about this for years and came up with four distinct ways of imagining or understanding God, then created an evaluation of each:

1) Idea of a supernatural God
2) Idea of a natural God
3) Idea of God as the whole Universe
4) God the idea

First, I tackled the idea of God as a supernatural God. That concept was pretty uncomfortable. I was so hesitant to say that the natural was incomplete and that a supernatural was necessary and real. Eventually, I had enough, ran out of patience with the idea of God as supernatural, and wrote a critique in that *Good Consideration* essay.

1. IDEA OF A SUPERNATURAL GOD
After the opening points about beliefs, I wrote this argument against the idea of a supernatural God.

WHAT IS GOD?
I should begin by defining what I mean by "God." The simplest definition is that God is the Almighty, the creator of the Universe, and the source of "good." He can do or be anything and has no limits. Wow! What a being I have

described! Could a being like this exist? I feel comfort in thinking there is a being that could have imagined, planned, and created all the beauties of the Universe. Sometimes I am struck by how amazing a spring day, for instance, is. It seems that this Universe, particularly human life here on earth, had to be created by a being that knew what it was doing. That God exists seems to fit my experience pretty well. It feels right.

Looking closer, though, I see problems with this idea. We could think of the God I described above of as *Separate from the Universe*. Picture the Universe as we normally think of it, including nature and man on one side, with God as a separate being on the other. An all-powerful, unlimited God of this type could play with the Universe any way he wished. In an instant, he could change all the basic laws of nature that we believe to be true. For example, something we know that is logically true in mathematics, $2 \times 2 = 4$, could be made to equal 5 if God chose to do so. If this type of God existed, any pursuit of knowledge here on earth would be a waste of time. Even this essay I am writing now would be pointless. There would be absolutely no understanding. Why bother learning something changeable based on the whim of God? This doesn't seem so right anymore.

There is another problem with this idea too. If God is the source of good, then anything that God does is good. God could change the laws of nature or destroy all life in an instant and this would be "good." This bothers me. I would rather think that "good" is constant and defined, not changeable or subject to the whim of God. Maybe this is my bias, but I like to think that "good" has priority over any concept of God. If this were the case, then God wouldn't really be almighty. It's hard to have it both ways.

Recently, I added to these views a logical argument that a supernatural God plus the Universe had to be greater than a supernatural God alone. We think of God as the creator and ruler of the Universe. God is a force that built and runs the Universe, a force that created something separate from itself that it dominates. Another way of saying it is the Universe is God's possession, but not God. Two things exist: God and the Universe. Given this view, wouldn't the sum of God and the Universe be more perfect and more complete than either separately?

God is not as powerful or complete as God plus the Universe, unless the Universe has no attributes, power, or value at all.

(Supernatural God + Universe) > Supernatural God

$$(GS + U) > GS$$

Does this statement imply that a supernatural God is incomplete? Unless the Universe is 0 or null, yes. Can I believe the Universe is 0? No, I cannot believe that. If it is 0, then I too am 0, and then the question becomes irrelevant. Also, what would that say about God? That he created and rules over nothing? No. God plus the Universe beats God alone. What is so fantastic about a supernatural God when it is not as grand as the Universe and supposed God-being combined?

Another reason I'm not a fan of the idea of a separate supernatural God is that I want to believe that the Universe operates rationally and can be knowable. A supernatural being that can interrupt natural processes is not desirable. It is definitely not simple or reasonable, and doesn't feel right. Also, there is the ethics aspect. Sometimes we view God as being perfect in goodness and the source of all moral authority. This is where it gets serious. We are talking about goodness and morality now. Are we comfortable handing over the keys to those words to a supernatural ruler, separate from the Universe, with perfect power? Are we willing to agree that God can say what goodness and morality are? I hope not. This has a scary, tyrannical feel about it. Fortunately, the general definition says he has perfect wisdom, too. Would perfect wisdom limit or constrain the options that a perfectly powerful ruler has to change what is moral and good? Would his perfect wisdom keep God from declaring that outright murder is a moral act? If wisdom can constrain or set boundaries on what is good or moral, then maybe wisdom is more powerful than we thought. Maybe goodness, morality, and wisdom come from something bigger than a supernatural God. If perfect wisdom has the power to limit the whims of a supernatural God-being, what is so special about the supernatural being, after all?

2. IDEA OF A NATURAL GOD

So, I would not believe in a supernatural God, but I still had a hard time walking away from the ideals of reverence, respect, and awe that filled my youthful Sunday mornings at church. I wanted something to be in awe of and revere in my daily life, so I tried a different route. I dug a little deeper into the idea of the word "supreme," as in supreme being. Synonyms for supreme include highest ranking, highest, leading, chief, head, top, foremost, principal, superior, premier, first, cardinal, prime. These words describe a ranking, hierarchical order. I wondered, Could we view God as the best of the Universe? God, not a supernatural one but a natural one, is the creator and ruler at the top of the Universe. The rest of the Universe is below. So, in this view, all of existence is the Universe, and God is the best part of it, but a part of it, not separate from it. Everything = Universe, and God is at the top of the Universe. At the bottom of the ranking are the least powerful, least wise, least good elements of the Universe. This understanding has God as the highest, utmost element of the Universe.

A God of this type is not a *separate* supernatural ruler of the Universe, but the best, most powerful *participant* within it. Here I am talking about a super being, one of unimaginable ability. The best, most powerful, wisest natural being. This being is the apex being. Given this view, the laws of the Universe still constrain God. This appeals to me. It seems reasonable to think there could be a being much more advanced than humans in abilities and attributes at the top of the Universe. This view characterizes God as a natural being, not a supernatural one, the epitome of ability in the Universe, but he is still part of the Universe, a natural part.

Similarly, in *Good Consideration* I wrote about this view.

I can think of another way of looking at the idea of God. This one I will call the *Top of the Universe*. Think of God as a being that is not separate from the rest of the Universe, but is the most Supreme Being within the Universe. Rather than a power different and outside the Universe, this being is the pinnacle or highest evolutionary being in the Universe. It has developed or strengthened to the point of mastery within the universal structure, within physical and logical boundaries. We're comfortable thinking of humans as the highest evolutionary being in the Universe, but try to imagine a Universe in which man is only the tiniest fraction of the way up the evolutionary scale. Imagine a being at the top. This being would appear to us to be God-like and would be nearly almighty. God is part of the Universe, is made of the same stuff, and playing by the same rules as me. I'm drawn to this idea because, with a God of this type, reason is still intact. I can continue with my essay and multiply 2 × 2. Furthermore, good would be independent of a God of this type. The problem with this concept shows up with worshipping this type of God. There is no reason to put a special value on a being that is still only a part of the Universe. No matter how exceptional or powerful a single being is, it can't be as grand or outstanding as the entire Universe combined. Why deem one aspect of the Universe to be God and leave out the rest when this one aspect is still a part of the whole? The characteristics of omniscience or omnipotence attributed to this being are also attributable to the Universe as a whole.

This idea depicts God as the most amazing part of the natural Universe. Pretty cool, but even this idea of God is not as grand as the full Universe with this natural God. This idea of God is the best part of the Universe, but still only part of the whole.

(Natural God + Remaining Universe) > Natural God Alone
(GN + Remaining U) > GN

3. IDEA OF GOD AS THE WHOLE UNIVERSE

Right after those words, I came to a major conclusion, one I accepted for a long time and only recently reconsidered. I thought there was a legitimate third option: God and the Universe are the same. I wrote about this in *Good Consideration*.

Instead of putting one part of the Universe on a pedestal and calling it God, I'm willing to put the entire Universe on a pedestal and think of the Entire Universe as God. I believe that the entire Universe is God. Everything that exists is part of God. Every bit of matter, every physical law, every thought and action is a part of the Universe and is part of God. God = Universe, Universe = God.

What a statement to make. I did not need to believe in a separate creator and ruler. Nor did I need to worship the topmost being. The Universe in its entirety is enough and is also God. God and the Universe are the same. God and Universe, no differentiation. This view aligned with those old notebook words on everything being natural, not supernatural, and yet allowed me to cling to a sense of God, or godly divinity.

The Universe is enough. All the things we love, admire, revere, and appreciate are in the Universe. I need not declare a belief in a God-being, either a supernatural one or a natural one. All the powers we are in awe of, the magic and mystery of life, are there in the Universe. Odd, barely understood phenomena we wonder about today may all exist, but if they do, they are part of the Universe, not separate. The pretty parts around us are not godlier than the ugly ones, the crooked not less godly than the straight. Morality is in the Universe too. I find ethics in how the Universe works and how life interacts with other life in ways that are varying degrees positive or negative. This is all about perspective. Let's call it what it is and avoid trying to conjure a supernatural or natural God-being. The Universe is plenty, and we should redirect our feeling of reverence toward the Universe, the world in which we are a part.

I wondered whether there is a godly part or aspect to the Universe and a part that is less godly. I concluded that godliness is homogeneous throughout the Universe. Every aspect of the Universe is 100 percent God. That seems illogical, but let me give an example. Imagine a coffee can filled with nuts, bolts, screws, and washers. These items are all made of 100 percent stainless steel. Though each item is unique, what they have in common is their metal. God is like the stainless-steel attribute that is elemental to each part, each item in the can.

This all sounded so brilliant. I thought I had found the answer. God could remain in my vocabulary because it was all of existence. My awe and reverence were intact. Divinity was everywhere. There is not a supernatural God that exists independently of the Universe. God is not a special, super part of the Universe, but God is the Universe through and through. There is a lot to like about this approach, but I don't think it is the entire answer.

4. GOD THE IDEA

In 1999, I wrote that God equaled the Universe, and I loved it. I thought it was my wisest insight ever. I held this view for a long time. Lately, I realized it was not as brilliant as I thought. I was trying to force it. I was trying to hold on to the idea of God in my life, but I overreached. Now, I have moved on from this view. One reason I needed to let this idea go is because the terms "God" and "a being" are inseparable. When people say God, they mean a being, an entity that is like a life but an all-powerful one. "Being" implies a character, a personality with the capacity for love, kindness, and vengeance. A God-being cares about us and wants us to do X, Y, or Z. That is not what I intended when I concluded God was the Universe. I wanted godliness in all the Universe, not a God-being, but these ideas are twinned. You say the word God and people hear "Supreme Being." They don't hear that everything in existence is supreme. I had forced my definition of God to meet my wish for godliness all around.

I also realized that if God is the Universe, then these two words mean exactly the same thing. Synonyms. God loses any distinction and becomes irrelevant. God becomes just another word for the totality of existence. If God 100 percent equals the Universe, then the meaning of God as a noun diminishes. No added value. If God is simply another word for the Universe, then what is the point? Why did I wrestle with this for much of my life? If God is fully the Universe, it is just a synonym. Have I pushed the idea of God to the point of irrelevance?

To move forward, I shifted the question of God to personal perspective or outlook. Instead of trying to say what God is, I focused on how we see the Universe, our lens or perspective. The question of God is not about God so much as it is about how we perceive the world. It is not about whether God exists. It is whether we can hold a point of view that reveres and respects the astounding Universe we take part in. What will our perspective on the Universe be? Can we look and see a world of majesty and awe that we can call totally fantastic, amazing? Can we revere it?

The answer is yes. I now think of God not as a being, supernatural or natural. God is not even a tangible thing. God is an idea, an idea we can apply to the highest and deepest elements of our human existence and awareness. I now see God as a term or expression. We can still include the word God in our vocabulary. We can think of the word God as the **Ultimate Adjective**. It is a descriptor—an adjective, not a noun. It says something about how we see existence, not what does or does not exist. God is an idea or ideal, not a tangible being. Think of the phrase "The Universe is God!" and substitute words like "Bitchin'" or "Gnarly" for "God" to get my meaning.

The Universe is Bitchin', the Universe is Gnarly, the Universe is God! God is a term. I am being flippant with those words, but I wanted to show that God is an expression.

What is the precise meaning of this adjective, God, the meta-adjective? Trying to define it leads me to think that God is the maximum and incomparable adjective. It is what we say when no other word or idea is adequate. It is a blend of human wish and hope wrapped in appreciation and gratitude. It is both warm and grand, humble and amazing. Fantastic multiplied by a factor of infinity and evidenced in the Universe. So, God exists, but not as we normally think of it. God is a human-made term we use to express our emotions and attribute value to what we perceive externally and what we feel and need internally. We revere what we see in the world around us, and we use the word God, the ultimate adjective, the unfathomable descriptor, for what we love, admire, and desire in our Universe!

Mystery comes to mind. We know a lot about how the Universe works, but the sum of our understanding is still tiny compared to the complexity and functionality that exists. I feel humble and reverential when I think about the wonders of the Universe and recognize that we understand only a small fraction. There is space for phenomena that we commonly think of as supernatural to occur naturally. These phenomena are just wrapped in mystery today. The mystery is appealing to me. I revere what we know and humbly honor the magnificence of what we can hardly conceive.

I love the idea of God because with it I connect to this mystery. God is the word we use to name, to share, our nearly unexpressible feelings of love, humility, joy, and awe when we acknowledge our small place and role in this limitless, grand Universe. We are human and we deal in what exists as actual phenomena. We also deal with our feelings and emotions as we live our lives. God is the expression we use to fill the void of the unknown that we perceive, that drives our highs and lows, strengths, and fears. God is an expression or term we can use when nothing else will do. The grandness of the Universe is more than any other word can express.

Accepting an idea of God as a term or expression has a practical side, too. When someone says the word God to me, I do not prepare an argument about there being no supernatural until we know the limits of what is natural. I don't go on the defensive or start laying out bullet points that would challenge the existence of God as a noun. When someone calls out to God, I hear them and appreciate where they are coming from and the human emotion and sense they are trying to express. I translate what they say about God to my understanding of God as a term or human expression.

I can be comfortable with the word God now because I translate it to my meaning of the word as an expression. This helps me hold on to that reverence and sense of wonder and majesty in the Universe that has been at my core my whole life. With this understanding of God, I get to use a vague but powerful and layered human term to capture so much about love, loss, hope, and awe that are part of the Universe and part of my life.

MY EVOLVING IDEAS OF GOD

1) Idea of a Supernatural God

This is the idea of the Catholic God I grew up with, the Holy Trinity God. A supernatural God could change the way the world works, change the laws of nature. In this paradigm, pursuing knowledge is useless because it all could change on a whim. Good, or morality, depends also on this supernatural being, so the foundations of right and wrong are subjective to the being and unknowable to us. Even if there is a supernatural God, the sum of God and the Universe is more perfect and more complete than God alone.

2) Idea of a Natural God

This is a different idea of God that proposes that God is not supernatural. God is the most advanced, amazing, and powerful part of the natural Universe. In this idea, natural laws are still valid and morality is rooted in the natural, which are appealing elements. Still, a God like this is not as grand as the full Universe.

3) Idea of God as the Whole Universe

The Universe in its entirety is enough and is also God. God and the Universe are the same. All the powers we are in awe of, the magic and mystery of life, are there in the Universe. If God is the Universe, then these two words mean exactly the same thing. God is another word for the totality of existence, all, the infinite Universe. If God 100 percent equals the Universe, then the meaning of God as a noun diminishes. It becomes a synonym for Universe. God, as something special, goes away.

4) God the Idea

God is an idea, a term or expression, the ultimate adjective. We can apply this word to the highest and deepest elements of our human existence and awareness. God is the word we use to name our nearly unexpressible feelings of love, humility, joy, and awe when we acknowledge our small place in this limitless Universe. God is the expression we use to fill the void of the unknown that we perceive, that drives our highs and lows, strengths, and fears as we go about our lives. God is the maximum and incomparable adjective. It is what we say when no other word or idea is adequate.

9

A LIFE ETHIC

Remember my earlier stories about how my dad and then brother cared for aged parents? Remember the tadpoles and brotherly kindness? My loved ones showed me right and wrong in how they lived. Experience tells me right and wrong surely exist. An ethics-less world goes against my grain. I believe actions are not all equal, and what we do matters. But how can we distinguish the good behaviors from the bad ones? What will we use as a guide? Clearly, I won't rely on the Bible to say what is right and wrong. Nor can I look to fear of sin or hell's damnation for the behaviors to avoid. I need to find a guide for morality in the non-supernatural. Any ethics we develop must be based on a non-supernatural-oriented foundation. No heavenly carrot or hell stick to drive me. To sort this out, I used the tools developed in the section on beliefs. Clarity, sensibility, and fit with my experience are the best measures to evaluate how to act ethically.

Using clarity, sensibility, and experiential fit, we can develop guides and principles to help us more often find and choose good behaviors. I returned to the Siena-era notebook to review what I wrote back then on ethics. These were scribblings in a notebook. They were rough, but they show how I worked on these topics back in my college days.

With there being no supernatural things, or at least nothing we can call certainly supernatural (one must know the bounds of the natural world before one can label something as beyond the bounds), we must look for the principles that guide our life to be rooted in the natural, things our mind can reason about and find truth in.

This means that the problem of moral behavior should focus on things or circumstances our minds can know. Morality should not be based on a supernatural goal but must tie itself to what is the object of our awareness. If morality, or any other principle of our life, does not do this, it risks deceiving itself. If deceived in this way, there is no way of knowing it.

* * * * *

Moral, or morality, seems to refer to a code or law. A moral decision is a decision that agrees with a principle of right and wrong. So, morality is a measure of right and wrong behavior. Morality is equal to right; wrong is immoral. Why is something right or wrong? Usually, the answer to this question is that God set the law of right and wrong. Well, how would my philosophy handle right and wrong without a typical concept of God? If God equals the Universe, can I say that the Universe itself set the law? Let's see. The Universe has everything in it. This includes the evil or destructive acts that occur every day. How can this be moral? There must be an answer here somewhere. If there is an answer, it must be in the Universe itself, not outside supernatural rules.

What principles do I see in the Universe that work? Morality is that which further advances the growth and development of the ~~Universe~~ "life". Now does this mean the entire Universe? If so, how can we possibly know whether an action of ours benefits or hurts the Universe? It may be good for some and bad for others. It may seem to be good, but in the long term will prove bad to the Universe. How can we tell? I would say it is difficult to tell what is good or bad for the entire ~~Universe~~ "life". All you can do is see what principles are good for the ~~Universe~~ "life" and measure our actions against those principles.

Later, in the *Good Consideration* booklet from 1999, I presented my views on morals and ethics. Below are my first ideas on an ethics based on the Universe, not the supernatural, not on sin, not on heaven or hell. I even avoid using the terms good and evil, since they are so loaded with supernatural tones and meanings. What you will find here is an honest attempt to center morality around behaviors that benefit the Universe.

Ethics is the study of morals and moral choices. It is a topic of philosophy that ventures into territory often claimed by religion. Obviously, my starting point on this topic is what I was taught in the Catholic Church. I learned God is the judge of right and wrong behavior and that the church helps people face moral decisions and act rightly. I think two main points of Christian moral behavior are (1) we should act the way Jesus did, be kind to others and follow his example of love; and (2) immoral actions are sins, and the accumulation of sins, without repentance, will cause our souls to be sent to hell in the afterlife.

The church offers two different motivations for moral behavior. First, we should do the right thing because it is the "right thing." An example of this is "We should help others just for the sake of helping others." I agree with this motivation for behavior. It is sensible and fits my experience well. The second motivation is not as good. This says we must be good so we will go to heaven, not hell, in the afterlife. The example here is "We should help others to ensure a place for ourselves in heaven." On the one hand, we are encouraged to be good for goodness' sake, and on the other we are encouraged to be good so we may go to heaven. Which is it? Maybe we are supposed to use motivation B when we are young and mature into motivation A.

Obviously, the heaven and hell motivation does not fit my philosophy. The "be good for goodness' sake" idea is better, but it leaves two questions. One, is there a set of behaviors that are absolutely "good" or right, and two, why would someone choose good or right over wrong? What's the motivation? Some people may say that "right and wrong" or "good" behavior really doesn't exist. They think that what is good for one person may be bad for another. For them, "good" is a relative and variable term, relative to the situation at hand and the people involved. This is the question I need to answer first. After that I'll move on to the second part, which deals with the motivation to choose good behavior.

Is there right and wrong in the Universe? I think the answer is yes. Let me clarify what I mean by right and wrong. I don't think actions clearly fall into categories or labels of right and wrong. Morality is not really an either/or situation. I'm not supporting relativism here. Right and wrong exist and are absolute, but they are on either ends of the behavior spectrum. Most actions lie somewhere between purely right and purely wrong. It's not an on/off, yes/no situation. To the extent that our actions support what is good, they are more or less moral, more or less right. Our goal is to try to behave as rightly and make as much of a positive impact as we can.

I think morality and right and wrong are appropriate only for living, not nonliving, parts of the Universe. Right and wrong and good and bad can only be defined in relation to life. There can't be a bad or immoral storm, wind, or flood. While these forces act upon us, they act without a moral component. There is no choice involved, just a combination of natural forces. Living beings, though, have some control over their actions. Intelligent species, with man being the most intelligent that we know of, obviously have more control over their actions than the primitive species, but even simple organisms respond to their environment in ways they have learned are successful. This response, and being able to control these responses, are key to what it means to be alive and throw one into the arena of right and wrong. Nonliving things don't make choices and don't drive their own actions; they are outside the sphere of morals.

Living things, any life, simply amazes me. Think about life for a minute and I'm sure it will amaze you, too. One thing I notice as I look at diverse types of life is that there is a similarity between living things. Trees, bugs, animals, and people in general try to exist, grow, and persist in their existence when faced with challenges. This common thread runs through all life. It may be a stretch, but it seems that all life has two things in common: some control over their own actions, plus the desire to exist and grow. The significance of this is that these two points together form the basis of my morality.

If all life has a desire to exist and grow and all life has some control over its own actions, then can I conclude that ethical behavior is controlling one's actions so they promote the existence and growth of life? That is quite a mouthful, so let me break this down a bit. Moral questions are appropriate only for living things. Living things have some control over their actions. Actions promote or detract from the existence and growth of life. Existing and growing is a common thread of life. We should act in such a way that our lives promote the existence and growth of life. Accordingly, the main moral principle is this: we should act to promote and support the existence and growth of life.

What does the phrase "promote the existence and growth of life" mean? Am I saying we should not harm any specific life? No, that wouldn't be possible. Every time we eat, we've harmed a life. Am I saying it's wrong to eat? No, I'm not saying that. Look at how we live. Everything we do affects other life in some way. We wash our hands and that kills bacteria. We walk in the yard and that damages the grass. All life interacts with other life in apparently violent and harmful ways. This is not necessarily immoral. In fact, in broad terms, life grows and develops because of this struggle and this give-and-take. What I am saying is we should promote the existence and growth of life in general. Our actions should promote and help bring about an environment where life, in general, will be more able to exist, grow, and thrive.

Now it's time to elaborate on this a bit. What behaviors or types of actions support the existence and growth of life, and how can we evaluate or judge behavior as fitting this concept or not? I think there is only one way to judge whether a behavior or action is good: good behaviors are those that, if performed by all life, would make the Universe a better place for life to exist and grow.

By using the phrase "all life," I say that what is good behavior for one is by necessity good behavior for another. The action is relevant, but the actor is not. It takes the specific and expands it to the whole to see whether a behavior is good or not. We can see this better by looking at an example. Stealing a car obviously seems like a terrible thing to do. By my test, which follows, it is also bad. First, what is the action? It is stealing a car. If all life acted this way, would the

Universe be a better place for life to exist and grow? I think not. A Universe filled with this type of behavior would be tough to survive in. This behavior is harmful to the existence and growth of life.

How does this work in practice? (1) Think of an action or behavior. (2) Think of what the Universe would be like if all life acted this way. (3) Judge whether this Universe would be a better place for life to exist and grow. "Better" can mean better than if no life acted this way or better than the Universe is today, whichever comparison is more appropriate.

I love the Life Ethic idea from this essay! It may be the most original and important idea I developed. This concept points us toward how we should try to act. What should we do? Act in such a way that if all life acted this way, the Universe would be a better place for life to exist and grow. I love it! It is simple and clear, seems reasonable, and fits with my life experiences. This Life Ethic is like a compass pointing north, and it is an indicator of a general direction for us to strive. It is not a set of step-by-step directions, but it is a good rule of thumb.

We should act in such a way that if all life acted this way, the Universe would be a better place for life to exist and grow. There are a couple of elements here. First, there is the "all life acted this way" element. It says there is equality among us. There is not one set of rules for some and different rules for others. This echoes the words of Immanuel Kant in his Categorical Imperative, in which he said, "Act only according to the maxim whereby you can, at the same time, will that it should become a universal law." It is the universal law part that we both have in common. I learned of the Categorical Imperative in a Siena philosophy class called Modern Continental Philosophy. The Categorical Imperative topic fascinated me.

The second part of my Life Ethic phrase is the object or goal of the behavior. Kant is not specific about what that universal law achieves. I add the outcome. I added a statement of what we should direct the behavior toward. It is an explicit goal, a goal of living your life in a way that if everyone acted similarly, the world would be a better place for life to exist and grow.

Ethics is about how we as individuals behave. We should ask ourselves what the world would be like if everyone performed an action. Would it be good? Would it be a world in which life has a better chance of flourishing? This is a strong ask. Good behavior is not about avoiding hell or pleasing God, hoping to win favor and a front-row seat in the afterlife. It is about our choices and the effects those choices have on others. By asking ourselves how the world would look if everyone did this same action, we can gain a measure of the action's ethical quality.

My Life Ethic statement differs vastly from a principle that pushes or forces outcomes. This is an important clarification. We should not set out to compel behaviors of others to achieve an ideal of what we think the Universe should be. A grade school teacher introduced me to the concept that the end doesn't justify the means. I liked it then and still do. We simply need to manage our own behavior and act in ways that if everyone acted that way, the Universe would be more likely to be fertile for life to thrive. We can advocate behaviors we think would make the Universe a better place for life to thrive. If everyone did this, the Universe would be a better place for life. The dialog would be beneficial. It is simple. We should influence, not implement; communicate and convince, not dictate. Using force to dictate or control other people's behavior is not all right. If everyone did this, the world would not be a better place for life to exist and grow.

I love the Life Ethic, but it is hard to use in real-life situations. The problem starts with "act," the first word. "Act in such a way that if all life acted this way, the Universe would be a better place for life to exist and grow." With this sentence, one has to ask, "What is an action?" An action may sound simple and obvious, but we can break actions down into components. We can then evaluate these components, or sub-actions, individually.

Let's look at an example: driving your child to school. This sounds simple and like a fairly good action. We can imagine a world with everyone doing this. That world feels OK. However, it gets more complicated if you break down the action into its components. What type of car are you driving—an SUV or hybrid? Is everyone buckled in? Are you speeding or driving distractedly? Is the school close to home and walkable? Gosh, this is a lot to consider. You'll be late for school if you stop to consider these aspects. Definitely not doable in real time. You can think about these elements later, maybe when you have time. Then you can consider these sub-actions fairly without getting lost in the minutiae or being overly self-critical.

Besides the challenge of isolating specific actions and evaluating the ethical aspects of each, there is another challenge when trying to put this principle into practice. It is all-encompassing. There is no off switch. I do not limit this Life Ethic principle to the classic moral questions, the purview of the Ten Commandments, for example. It applies to all our actions. Our every action is subject to personal moral evaluation—simple things like making breakfast or skipping it; returning a call or passing; speaking out or staying silent; paper, plastic, or reusable. These all have moral aspects. The Life Ethic is all-inclusive. No part of our life is exempt. Our whole life is subject to personal scrutiny on a moral scale, and that is unwieldy and impossible. We could run scenarios and more scenarios, constantly imagining what would happen if everyone in these exact circumstances acted that way. This isn't doable. There are too many actions to process. Taking the Life Ethic to its full extent, applying it to our every breath and action, would be paralyzing.

The Life Ethic is a great general guide but impossible to practice at the smallest action level. It is directional and aspirational. We need to temper the Life Ethic with common sense, judgment, and grace. I think the way to manage this is to focus on the essence or most significant aspect of the action. Don't get lost in the details and connected elements.

Recently Carolyn, Sammy, and I were in our car headed to lunch. The car was an SUV, not a hybrid. I was not speeding or driving distractedly, and the restaurant was beyond walkable. Suddenly, we saw two lost dogs walking down the side of a busy road. I was unsure what to do, but Sammy knew. Her gut told her to see whether we could help these lost dogs. I turned off the road and, with a few right turns, made it back to the dogs. Sammy opened the door and leaped out, calling gently to the pups. I parked, and the dogs came to us. One was big, the leader; the other hung by his side. Someone had cared for these dogs. They had collars and rabies tags. Carolyn jumped to action and contacted the vet, then the owner, and they came and picked up the dogs. It worked out well. We felt so good.

The essence of the activity was that we saved two dogs that were roaming loose on a busy street. This is something that, if done by everyone, would make the world a better place. Without Sammy in the car, I may have failed to do this. I hesitated, but she knew in her heart what to do. Helping the dogs was the essence of the activity. The question of the car type, the quality of my driving, and the issue of walkability are distractions. We can consider these at some point, but the situation called to us, and with Sammy's help, we heard it and acted. The essence of the activity was saving the dogs. My morality uses hundreds of words to construct what her heart knew instantly.

It is wise to use the Life Ethic as a tool to evaluate the big choices we have that would make the Universe a better place. Focusing on the essence of the actions is a step in the right direction.

Writing *Good Consideration*, I struggled with how to put the Life Ethic into practice.

For example, if a doctor and a banker both live their individual lives aligned with the principles above, which one benefits the existence and growth of life more? Possibly the doctor, because he is involved with healing and promoting health. On the other hand, the banker may be generously and fairly providing loans to needy applicants. How can one judge which type of life one should lead? What about a person who volunteers all their time to charity versus one who raises three kids in the suburbs? Which life is better? Both people may follow good principles in their daily interactions, but is that enough? Shouldn't we also try to make our occupations and vocations be the type that promote the existence and growth of life?

I think the answer to this question is yes. The problem is there is not a single occupation that, if performed by everyone, would make the Universe a better place for life. The Universe benefits from a diverse mix of occupations. Knowing this, how can we decide what to pursue? The first thing we should do is evaluate what skills and interests we have and pick a way of life that can fully use our skills and provide for our own growth and satisfaction. If everyone in the Universe did this, the Universe would be a better place for life to exist and grow. The second step is to evaluate the options we have in leading our lives and creating the type of life that contributes most. This is where our specific skills meet a universal opportunity. The life we choose should not sacrifice our own existence or growth. We must remember that for a type of life to be good, it must still be good if all life acted or lived this way. Thus, it requires us to choose lifestyles thoughtfully and intelligently.

I have written a lot about nature in this book, so I want to explore how nature fits with this Life Ethic proposal. Is nature special? By nature, I mean everything that is not human-made. Nature is brutal and apparently heartless, but most interactions within nature are one on one. These are limited in scope. A creature eats and a creature dies. The need or urgency of an individual to continue to exist seems to drive actions.

Carolyn and I were sitting out by the quiet pool in Orange Beach when a nature drama unfolded before our eyes. We were quietly reading, minds wandering, when we saw a three-inch lizard creep out from the bushes and slip out onto the concrete tiles of the pool patio. Creep isn't exactly right. It hustled then froze, hustled then froze. About five feet from the bushes, taking in the warm sun, he shifted his head and snapped something up in his mouth. I am not sure what he ate, but I suspect it was an ant. Boom! In an instant, he took a life and converted it to food. He remained there for a few minutes, exposed in the sun and probably feeling rather good about his hunting, when drama number two happened. A mockingbird popped out of a nearby tree, swooped down in a flash, snatched him up, and disappeared back into the tree. We let our books drift down to our chests as we turned to each other and said, "Did you see that?" We were stunned. That is how life works, but to see it play out in front of you is something.

While this was hard to watch, we did not feel bad or think it had significant negative ethical considerations. Each creature has a right to sustain itself. In simple terms, this behavior fits with the morality views presented above. Did either of these creatures act in such a way that if all creatures did this, the Universe would not be a good place for creatures to exist and grow? No. These scenes are raw, but I think they are OK.

It is the non-nature parts of existence where the potential for large-scale horror and immorality exists. Non-nature includes anything artificial or human-made. This is our domain. While we are of nature, we expand beyond nature because we create and fabricate ideas and things. Through our intelligence, we leverage our presence and influence way beyond our one-on-one interactions. Concepts, prejudices, and rages develop and spread. Some of these may be destructive on a global scale. We use devices and inventions to multiply our power further still. Humanity has unbelievable power, and the range of our actions is unlimited. Given these factors, it is clear that ethics is extremely important to humanity. Humans are way too powerful to have weak foundations for ethics. We need to get a handle on what is ethical and what is not. With humans having such power, this is a top priority. Thousands of years of religious approaches to morality have not accomplished the task of finding a broadly ethical way for us to live. It is time for some fresh thinking. Though somewhat limited in day-to-day use, the Life Ethic is a great lens from which to evaluate our actions and frame the discussion of ethical behavior.

10
ETHICS PRINCIPLES

The Life Ethic provides direction on what we should aim for in our actions. But it is difficult to work with day to day. To offer something more manageable than the Life Ethic, I selected the following six principles as ideals or outstanding characteristics for us to live by. I selected these principles based on how well each one fits with the Life Ethic goal. I am expressing these in adjective form, so they read as, I am...

Aware—knowing that something exists, or having knowledge or experience of a particular thing

Compassionate—having sympathy and empathy for the suffering of others and a wish to help them

Generous—willing to give money, help, kindness, and the like

Positive—full of hope and confidence, or giving cause for hope and confidence in others

Truthful—honest and not containing or telling any lies

Vital—full of life and energy and the will and power to persevere

These six principles are debatable. Others could develop different sets of principles and we can discuss and debate how good each principle is based on how each one aligns with the Life Ethic. I think these principles are pretty clear, make sense, and align with my experiences. These six, working together, make the world a better place for life to exist and grow.

I organize these six principles into three groups. The first group is compassion and generosity. These go together because they center on our relationships with others, which is often the first thing we think about when we consider ethics. Second, grouped together are positiveness, truthfulness, and vitality. These are together because they represent our disposition or general approach to how we conduct ourselves, how we spend our minutes on this planet. The third group is awareness, which interacts with and coordinates all the others.

COMPASSION AND GENEROSITY

Compassion is concern for the sufferings of others. Generosity is doing what you can to ease those sufferings. Compassion is feeling it, generosity is doing something about it—meaningfully giving of yourself and your resources. These both are outward-facing principles that begin with feeling, then move to action, kind action, toward others. Compassion is valuable even though it seems less tangibly beneficial than generosity. Compassion strengthens the connection and respect between lives. It is a prerequisite to being a wonderful human. If everyone acted with compassion, the Universe would certainly be a better place for life to exist and grow.

Compassion recognizes that many people are less fortunate than us and we feel emotion about that. Generosity is the action side of compassion. Compassion is recognition. Generosity is extending the helping hand. Compassion calls and generosity responds. Generosity helps relieve and improve the situations of those in need.

Some may argue that my choices of compassion and generosity are bad choices. They may say that others get what they deserve and use classic phrases like "Made your bed, now lie in it" or "Pull yourself up by your bootstraps." These phrases don't ring true to me. It is a trap for the rugged individualist in me to think that the playing field is equal for us all, that I am fully, 100 percent responsible for my own success and others are fully responsible for their own hard circumstances. I can pat my back all day long for my accomplishments. The thing is, we are all not starting from the same place and the playing field is not level. Lately, I have realized how unequal the playing field is. There are lots of causes, but one is the economic circumstances into which one is born. While we were not rich in our house growing up, we never lacked food, clothing, or education. We were not economically fast-tracked like the truly wealthy, but when my brothers, sister, and I were born, we did not start off far behind.

Let's take a closer look at economic disparity at birth and how this factor creates an uneven playing field and makes the principles of compassion and generosity so essential. This may be an odd way to look at it. But let's contrast baby humans with lion cubs. A newborn lion is quite similar to another, and so is the lion's pride similar to other prides. Each animal's ability to survive and thrive differs slightly, but lion cubs are very similar, and so are the prides of which they are a part. Lions have sharp teeth, claws, keen eyesight, a strong sense of smell, and well-developed muscles. These attributes set the power of the lion to thrive in the world. This is the same with other animals. Their physical attributes determine their power.

For humans, physical attributes are important but not the key attributes that help us succeed. Our physicality does not truly limit our power. It is money. Babies look alike. They are physically similar, but the bank accounts of their families will make enormous differences in their lives.

I did a little exercise with the help of Google Search. I typed into the search bar "median world wealth per person." It came back with the number $8,360. I then typed in "number of millionaires in the world," and it gave me 56.1 million. Last, I typed "number of billionaires in the world," and I got 2,640. The reason for this Googling was that I was looking for a visual way to illustrate the extremely unequal wealth aspects of the world's population. These wealth inequalities call into question the veracity of the phrase "Everyone is created equal."

For this visual representation, assume that $10K of individual wealth equates with a being that is six feet tall, a physical stature attribute, height, something we all can relate to. I used $10K rather than the Google-supplied median of $8,360 for simplicity. The median is what you get if you line up all the individuals in the world according to wealth and select the one in the middle. This person has, call it, $10K in wealth and is six feet tall. That person has more economic power than the nearly half the world's population below. Visually, this would show less-wealthy people standing less than six feet tall, some very tiny, a percentage only inches high. If someone in the wealthy half had $100K of wealth, like many in the developed world, they would be sixty feet tall and looking down upon the shorter, less powerful population. The 56.1 million millionaires, slightly under 1 percent of the population, assuming they all have just one million each, stand at six hundred feet tall! These are freaking giants, so much more powerful than the six footers. How tall would the 2,640 billionaires be? A billion dollars of wealth puts you at six hundred thousand feet tall, 113.6 miles high! These people are beyond giants. Who knows what you would call them? Gods?

That analysis looked at individual wealth. There is another player to consider—corporations. Some are moderately sized, but some are super wealthy. Apple and Microsoft, among the largest, have market caps near, or over, $2.5 trillion. That $2.5 trillion equates to a height of 284 thousand miles. These entities duck when the moon goes by. The moon is about 240 thousand miles away. It is unfathomable how entities of this stature tower over humans, even the tallest (wealthiest) ones. In addition, corporations are not mortal. They sometimes end in bankruptcy or other terminations, but they do not have a finite life. Wow, these are quite the artificial entities we have created.

Being born into a poor home makes life much more challenging. At our birth, we are not all equal. Some babies land in the arms of wealthy giants, some land with very limited financial support. We need to recognize this inequality and do what we can to make less powerful lives better. We can honor a way of life that believes in rugged individualism, but we should not use that value to beat or diminish others. Our principles of compassion and generosity guide us to act in ways that help the "smallest" in height, to support the chance for a good life for everyone. It is not OK to assume that every person has the same chance at financial stability and success.

My mom comes to mind when I think of compassion. Her heart was boundless. She deeply felt the hardships of the world and was the opposite of cold or self-centered. Along similar lines, the quality of generosity goes to my aunt Margaret. Margaret never married or had children and directed her kindness toward her nieces and nephews. She gave me her time, interest, and love. She was generous with everyone I knew. Plus, she was a kindergarten teacher, which is a super generous vocation.

POSITIVENESS, TRUTHFULNESS, AND VITALITY

I debated whether to include the principle of positiveness. I didn't want to suggest we should put on a disingenuous face of positivity. Positivity is more about how we influence others. We should be like cell phone chargers for others. We charge them up when we interact with them. After engaging with us, they come away feeling that they can do more, be more, than they thought they could. It is us simply making a positive mark, being a positive influence on others. My inspiration for keeping positive as a guiding principle is that it is part of the message of the Prayer of Saint Francis, a prayer I have loved since I was a child. That prayer does not say it explicitly, but the words imply that where one finds a negative, one should contribute positively to remedy it.

Being a positive influence on others requires maturity. Wisdom supplies context about how life works and helps us better gauge what is really happening.

With wisdom and a positive orientation, we can see the negative events that happen to us all and recognize them for what they are, probably manageable turns rather than the horrible monsters we sometimes see them as being. Even when events are horrible monsters, there often will be a way to deal with them that, when considered, may offer hope. That is what positivity means to me.

My uncle Leo embodied positivity. He always had a vibe about him that left you feeling better about yourself. His positivity seemed genuine. The way he interacted with me made me feel valuable and seen. His positivity was contagious. I smile now, thinking of him.

The next principle on my list is truthfulness. My career has been in accounting, and I admire the discipline because we are the truth tellers in the organization. It falls on us to present accurately the financial conditions we see. I was always prepared to be fired rather than misrepresent numbers. This does not make me special. It is the essence of the role, and nearly everyone I worked with saw it this way. Many times, I had to report unwelcome news, a much bigger loss than expected, a control failure, something like that. Accept the failure, own it, and take responsibility. That is what I had to do. In addition, I needed to figure out what happened and prevent it from happening again. There was no dodging it, even when the circumstances were difficult.

I feel fortunate to have had a career and direct supervisors who encouraged and supported personal integrity. From mill controllers I worked for back when I was a new accountant on the scene to the CFO I worked with for over two decades, the expectation was that we acted with integrity and honesty. We faced many high-pressure challenges and, even then, there was no direct or implied pressure to bend the rules or express something that was not true. I am grateful for this leadership and work environment.

Being truthful is so important. Recognizing something actually is a certain way, an objective, factual way, is especially important in creating an environment of trust as well as an environment where people can collaborate and society can advance. Lying and misrepresenting the facts of a situation are simply not OK. These behaviors work against creating a world in which life can exist and grow.

I have gotten so mad at the disregard for truth in media and social media over the last several years. People spread misinformation intentionally to get results they want. This phenomenon is not new, but it certainly seems more common now. How does one know what to believe? This common disregard for truth makes everything feel shaky and unsettled. It is hard to be sure of the facts now because people present false information as equivalent to truthful information in so many areas. We must change our ways to appreciate the value of truthfulness. Each of us needs to restrain from spreading falsity, even if that falsity might seem to help us in the near term.

My dad was a super example of truthfulness. He was what you'd call a straight arrow. He personified this principle by making truthfulness a part of his identity. Being truthful leads to being trustworthy. Living this way helps make the Universe a better place for life to exist and grow.

The last principle of the three is vitality. This is living a life of action, passion, and energy rather than passivity and listlessness. We need to be alive when we are alive. I talked earlier about seeing ourselves as individuals and portions of the entire Universe. This made me realize the Universe needs all of us individuals to be fully alive. The Universe benefits if the self does what it is supposed to do. The most basic "supposed to do" task we have is self-care. You Infinite (I) benefits if You Finite (F) take care of yourself. You (I) needs You (F) to take care of You (F) because that, at the most basic level, is what You (I) expects and what You (I) benefits from. You (I) needs You (F) to do your job, live to your capability.

The Universe needs you to be vital. Do your job. Be healthy, be smart, be as able as you can, flourish. Use your attributes and characteristics. The Universe outfitted you for what it expects of you. Get in touch with your abilities and activate them. Use the resources you need—you may do this, and the Universe expects it from you. Do not take more than you need. Do not self-destruct. Serve the needs of You (I).

Revisiting the cell and organism analogy, what helps the organism the most is for the cell to do its job. The organism needs each cell to do its job, simple as that. A bone cell, a blood cell, a brain cell—each has its own attributes and using those attributes helps the organism thrive. None of these cells are inherently unworthy or flawed. They just are, and the organism needs each to do its job and to be vital. The organism benefits if a cell does its job exceedingly well, becomes the best cell it can be, fulfills its nature based on its inherent characteristics, attributes, and so on. The organism suffers if the cells fail at doing their job. A weak and failing cell is not doing its job for the organism. Conversely, in a case of cancer, certain cells go rogue. They do not do their job. They go off on their own. This harms or destroys the organism. A cell is to an organism as a person is to the Universe is an analogy, but it is insightful and helpful in thinking about ethics and how we should see ourselves.

Languishing in a weak state is not ideal, but gosh, have I languished the last few years. From COVID-19 through political polarization, global conflicts and war, commonplace meanness, bigotry, and environmental destruction, any aware and truthful person would be horrified by the state of the world and what humanity has done to one another and to our planet. It is so disheartening, depressing. Honestly, this all works against the principle of acting with vitality.

These times can pull up the most hopeless feelings that erode vitality. At times like these, vitality is simply persisting forward despite the ugly facts that confront us. It is finding ways to choose more fit behaviors and not give in to despair. It is finding ways to act, however small, that express and use our capabilities. Vitality, especially when things look bleak, is hard but worth pursuing.

Choosing someone who personifies vitality is tough. Everyone embodies it occasionally. There is one group of family members who exemplified this characteristic every time I spent time with them. These are the Bradleys in Long Island, the family of my mom's brother Arthur. Their household seemed so full of life and energy when we visited Arthur when I was young. Arthur was severely limited physically because of a stroke, but he and the rest of the family had a powerful energy, warmth, directness, and love. This made his vitality, and that of the family, more poignant.

AWARENESS

Awareness is indispensable. Awareness of the conditions of others around us, and awareness of the way our actions affect others, is great. This principle also serves a role in balancing the other five principles. Awareness is like the quarterback who sees the field and the moving players and makes the play. For instance, we cannot employ truthfulness and positivity 100 percent of the time. Sometimes being truthful is inconsistent with high positivity and we need situational awareness. It would be fake and insincere to be positive all the time. Awareness gauges the situation and helps one use these principles wisely.

Awareness comes into play so much. Should we generously give to others to the point we ourselves do not have money and become needy? This is tricky. We need awareness to help find the balance we can live with. Awareness helps us to strive for a high amount of compassion and generosity, but an amount that is not so high that we significantly hurt ourselves.

The example of awareness goes to my wife, Carolyn. She is aware of the wake she makes in the world and tries to be careful with those waves. We have a term we use—her mom coined it—called HUB. This is "Head Up Butt." Often you see people who appear to be clueless about others or the effects of their actions. Carolyn is the opposite of a HUB.

* * *

I am so thankful to have had these people in my life, and I appreciate the life lessons they gently taught me through their own way of living. If my mom read this morality section, she would say that my ethics are a fancy way to say love. Love one another. Love, love, love. She would be right. I developed a way of saying much the same thing that she showed daily.

My ethics also reflect the influences of morality with which I was raised. These include the Ten Commandments, the Eight Beatitudes in Matthew, the description of love from the Bible—1 Corinthians

13. Beyond this there is the Prayer of Saint Francis. These are all religious but there are other elements too, some more secular ideas such as the Golden Rule and the words in "Desiderata." There is even a *Star Trek* point of view about group needs outweighing the needs of the few in a conversation between Spock and Kirk in *Star Trek II: The Wrath of Khan*. Clarity, sensibility, and rings true with my experience all play a part in development of these ethics views.

11
ETHICS EXTRA

ETHICS CHART—A FALSE START

The *Good Consideration* essay was full of thoughts on morality. I was probably obsessed with the idea. More than anything, I wanted to create an ethical way to behave that did not depend on church theology. Occasionally, that led to insights like the Life Ethic. In other cases, it led to dead ends. Below is a dead end, but an interesting one. When I wrote this, I thought I was on to something special, but after living with it for a while, I decided it was overly analytical and mechanical. I am presenting it to show how ideas pop up, take the stage, then sometimes need to be escorted off. This is one of those that I dropped, the Ethics chart.

I came up with a different way of looking at the impact of our actions on us and the rest of society. It is an overly technical way of looking at it, but I think it makes an excellent illustration. Every action we make has some level of personal, immediate value to ourselves, and we can plot this impact on a vertical line or y-axis. Positive numbers are personal gains, and negative numbers are losses. The dots represent specific actions. Eating might be a 2 on the scale, sleeping might be 1, and harming ourselves might be a –2. The scale here is not important. What is important is that certain actions benefit us more than others. We can plot these actions on a vertical line. Similarly, a horizontal line, x-axis, can be drawn that represents the short-term gain or loss to society. Less short-term societal gain on the left, more short-term society gain on the right. Since every action we make has both personal and societal effects, it makes sense to combine these two lines into an X, Y chart. This drawn chart has four quadrants and I'll describe each.

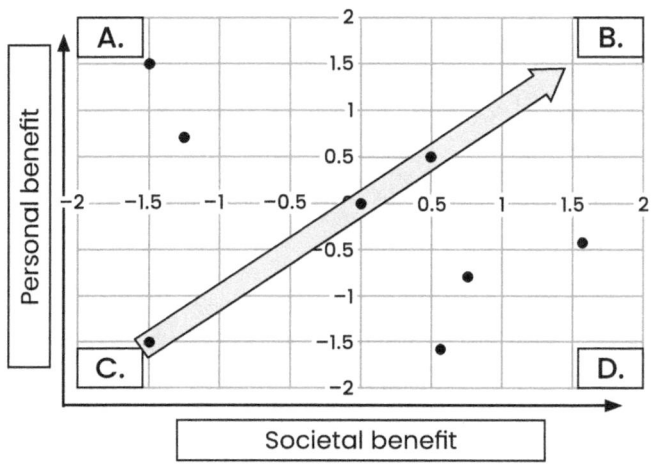

A) Positive personal impact, negative societal impact

Behaviors in this box benefit the individual in the short term, but they do this at the expense of the rest of society. Behaviors in this box offer no mutual support or compassion between people.

B) Positive personal impact and positive societal impact

This is the best box for our actions to be. Behaviors in this box support the existence and growth of life by matching immediate personal gain with direct societal gain.

C) Negative personal impact and negative societal impact

Behaviors in the box offer no value to either the individual or society. They are the least ethical behaviors possible. They are opposed to the existence and growth of life.

D) Negative personal impact, positive societal impact

This box represents behaviors that are self-sacrificing. Behaviors in this box have short-term value to society but have a detrimental impact on the individual. In the long run, behaviors that benefit society at the expense of the individual are not sustainable. It is hard to see that life would truly benefit if all life acted this way.

What behavior should we be striving for? Obviously, behaviors in box B seem the most moral. They provide for the continued existence of the individual plus positive benefits to society. To be honest, a question remains as to why someone would not simply choose behaviors high up the y-axis regardless of the societal impact. Why should someone care about the societal impact? My answer comes down to the difference between short-term gain and long-term best interest. Behaviors that are high up the y-axis, but are detrimental to society, will generate a short-term personal gain but will eventually weaken and deteriorate the environment in which the individual lives. This would not be in the individual's long-term best interest. Truly selfish behavior demands a compromise between the individual and society in the short term. I believe people who are truly looking out for their own long-term interests will try to make their actions benefit both themselves and society in the short term.

Behaviors that balance our own immediate gains with immediate societal gains are the most ethical. They promote the long-term benefit of the individual and society and promote the existence and growth of life. Behaviors on the diagonal line, and as far out as possible, are the best or most ethical since they support the individual and society.

Since I wrote this, I have concluded that I am not a fan of this ethics chart approach. A well-lived life that includes ethical behavior is not the intersection of personal and societal behavior transactions. In addition, we do not know what is truly good for us or good for society. We can fool ourselves and end up being harmful while thinking we are being moral. I included this ethics chart to show the extent of my struggle with finding a solid footing for morality that is not based on the supernatural. I also included it because it shows that I am fine with thinking of something, putting it on paper, then, after consideration, letting it go.

MORE

In *Good Consideration*, I asked several other questions about ethics and morality. I asked whether self-sacrifice was a moral aim. I wondered about whether morality at its root was behavior that produced the most benefit. These are legitimate questions.

What about altruism and self-sacrifice? I don't think self-sacrifice is a good motivation for behavior. This was a tough conclusion to accept because the church I was raised in recognized value in sacrifice. We had the season of Lent in which they encouraged us to give up something we loved to appreciate the sacrifices that Jesus made. As a kid, I would pick something such as giving up gum or chocolate for those weeks. I never could see how this was good or holy. It made me feel as though I was doing good because it was tough, like work, but it didn't benefit anyone. Perhaps it benefited me because I became more aware of the condition of people who don't have what I have—gum or chocolate. I suppose that is true. That being the case, it wasn't really self-sacrifice at all, just a subtle long-term growth opportunity.

Look at the idea of self-sacrifice through my ethics analysis. If all life in the Universe had self-sacrifice as a behavior motivation, the world would not be a better place for life. All life would pursue ways to detract from their own growth and existence. This would not be good.

Now I am not saying sacrifice is bad. I am saying it can be a means to a good end, not the end in itself. Don't sacrifice for the sake of sacrifice; sacrifice a short-term aim for the long-term goal of promoting the existence and growth of life. Promoting the existence and growth of life includes promoting the existence and growth of one's own life.

Am I saying that moral actions are those that benefit the Universe the most?

There is an important distinction here. Some people would advocate a morality that looks at the net impact of one's actions on the Universe. They would say that providing the most good to the greatest number is the highest morality. My concept of morality is different. I think a moral choice is one that would still be moral or benefit the existence of life if everyone acted that way. For example, dedicating one's life completely to serving others would not be moral, to me, if it meant degrading one's own life or growth. The reason is that if all beings did this, existence and growth of life would not be improved, just moved from one party to the next. This is a fine difference but, I think, a valid one. I am advocating a morality that would work for everyone, long term, not a solely need/benefit-driven morality.

Constructing an ethical framework is easier than living it. Let's first consider the Life Ethic. Live in such a way that if all life acted that way, the Universe would be a better place for life to exist and grow. This principle is very general. It is hard to know how well I am following this goal. I am mindful of this principle and think of it periodically, but it is hard to say whether I am consistent. Let's just say I try. There are some specific examples that show following this morality guide is difficult. A few years ago, I was on a ski trip with some family members and waiting at the Salt Lake City airport parking lot playing a word game, talking, waiting for friends to arrive. A man approached our car. He came to my side, the driver's side, and startled me. He looked distraught, or maybe sketchy, and then waved something in his hand. Jumper cables. I signaled him away like we couldn't help him. What the heck? I had two men with me in the car. This man was not likely to hurt us. Why was my first reaction so fearful and unkind? Is this the type of action that, if chosen by all life, would make the Universe a better place to exist and grow? No.

Another example is when deerflies pestered me to no end one day while I was running through the paved backcountry trails by the beach. These were small triangular flies with camo-looking wings. One landed on my arm, and I smashed it dead. I could have brushed it away. Why did I kill the fly when a brush-off would do? Does a fly's life matter in the morality I propose here? Is this the type of action that, if chosen by all life, would make the Universe a better place to exist and grow? No. It is not a horrible action, but maybe I should use only the force I need to protect myself, even from flies.

Next there is the set of six principles: be aware, compassionate, generous, positive, truthful, vital. One principle that I feel I could improve upon is generosity. Lately, I have been thinking that I could do more to support compelling causes. I give some money to charities, but I could do more. I don't go to church so do not donate there. At my prior employer, I gave to United Way. Here, we don't have that working through payroll deductions. I tip very well, but that helps only so much. I also do not currently volunteer much. This is a miss on my part. I need to find several organizations serving worthy causes and contribute my time and money to these.

The ethics described here explain what to strive for, why it matters, and which principles to apply. The trick is to do it consistently and make these practices part of my everyday thought process and life. Without being overly critical, I can honestly say I can do better. Maybe that is how life is. Know better, do better—continually regrouping toward higher possibility and improvement. I will regroup around these ethical points and pursue them with the passion and drive that I know I have.

PREDETERMINED OR FREE WILL?

Creating a moral or ethical framework implies that we have agency. We get to control to some degree our actions, and certain actions are better than others. We have choices and can drive our behavior toward the better ones. Sometimes, I have wondered whether this is the case. Could it be that things are predetermined? Is there a chance that we are living out a pre-set script? What comes to mind is a music player that shows graphically a song as a line and a dot on that line as the current point in time, the current point in the song. The song already exists in full. We experience each particular moment of the song only as the dot moves along. Past, present, and future are indistinguishable in a single block of existence, and we move through it.

I thought more about time and how we move from moment to moment. One day, I was walking Bradley down the sidewalk in our neighborhood toward a large oak tree a couple of blocks ahead. Our stepping feet beat out a cadence of time. As we walked forward, I wondered whether that tree ahead already exists in the future—say, a minute from now—when we get there because it is all preset. Even our walk was predetermined. The tree is there, unseen, waiting for the moment of experience to arrive. This portrays existence as a set thing, and each moment plays out along that set structure. Like the song example before, in this case, everything is predetermined. The moments are already there waiting to present themselves. Each moment takes the stage and then leaves as the dot moves along. This idea is very uncomfortable for me. There is no life, no animation, in this view. If reality is predetermined, then any discussion of morality or ethics is a waste of time. We have no control, no ability to influence anything. We just act out the notes on the preexisting song as each comes up. Everything is preset and running mechanically. This is quite uncomfortable, and I don't like this view.

Staring at that tree as we approached it, I wondered, What is the present exactly? How long in duration is "now"? We like to think of now as a moment, an hour, day, or week, an experience. The past, they say, is gone, and the future is not in existence yet, so the present, or now, is all there is. Does this mean that the present is all that exists? If so, how spacious is the present or now? If the present is only an instant, say a tenth of a second, then the word "now" can't exist as a whole. Just saying the word "now" takes about a second. The N sound can exist, then the O sound, then the *W* sound, all in sequence. "Now" can't exist, but only the parts can, as each successive instant appears. Are you feeling the earth shrink up under your feet as the present feels smaller and smaller?

Taking this to the extreme, I imagine an atom with electrons spinning or orbiting around the nucleus. With the view of reality described above, there is no spinning or orbiting of electrons, only the current positions of the electrons relative to the nucleus. The next instant will appear, and the electrons will be in different places. There is no movement within reality, as that would mean reality has both a past and a present. You can compare the state of "now" to a memory of a past thing, but you cannot compare a "was" and an "is" in existence at the same time because "was" is history, gone. Can the present be a razor's edge splitting past from the future? Is reality just the instantaneous present, a narrow line zipping forward in time?

This razor's edge view of reality as the instantaneous present is not OK with me either. I really don't feel comfortable with this view of reality. That reality is a thin microsecond line. There must be continuity from one moment to the next. What other options are there? How about the view that the past stays in existence as each layer of the present is added? Like rings of a tree that layer out with each passing year. The past is not gone, we just can't influence it. That tree we walked toward did not flash into existence zillions of times as moments flashed. That is ridiculous. The answer is simple. Each *now* is layered on top of all the earlier ones to form reality. Reality is built bit by bit. It encompasses all the previous bits or moments and includes each new one added on. The past exists and is continually being expanded by layers and layers of the present added on. Taken a little further, the past and the present are both reality, both exist, and are not significantly differentiated. The only difference between the reality of the past and the reality of the present is the ability for us to act on it. The present, or the now, is defined by our ability to influence or act on it. If we have an influence on it, it is present. If not, it is past, but both exist. This view is appealing.

Reality, existence, has a frontier, an edge, the present moment. That frontier continually expands at the pace of time, the pace of change. It is not all predetermined; existence is also not moment-to-moment flashing instances of the present. Reality is cumulative and influenceable in the present. Because of this, we should influence our *now*.

Carolyn and I were running one morning in Collierville, an early morning running date. We had known each other for only a short time. Agreeing to meet your hoped-to-be girlfriend at a neighborhood telephone pole at 5:30 a.m. is a sure way to get going early and avoid the snooze button. Now that she, my beautiful wife, is next to me in bed, it is more appealing to turn over and hug her than it is to head outside at that hour.

We were running along, about a mile in, and she told me about a scene she saw along the San Francisco

Marathon course when she ran that race. She described this as we were easing down the greenbelt path in the dark. "There was a train car in a field with a sign that said, 'Now is all you have.'"

Well, when she said this, I nearly lost a step and felt my air suck in. My gosh. After the deaths of Evelyn and Tom in 2008 and my divorce the year prior, I had been living those words in my daily life. Talk about ringing true. I thought, Gosh, this girl gets it.

I like to think the past stays in existence as each layer of the present is added. The only difference between the reality of the past and the reality of the present is the ability for us to act on it. We act in the present, the now. As the sign said, now truly is all you have. It is all you can take part in, and it is the part of reality you can do something with. Both the past and present exist, but the present matters most. Its length, whether it is a moment or a day, is irrelevant. The point is this: The now is your canvas, your playground, your untouched spreadsheet, waiting for your input. It is the classic screen with the green blinking cursor waiting for a keystroke. Move that cursor, throw the ball, take the step, make the call, do something with your now. Use the self-directed part of your identity to do what you can do to live life. Take advantage of your now!

12
SUMMARY

EVERYTHING IS NATURAL, THERE IS NO SUPERNATURAL

Everything is natural, there is no supernatural. I won't believe in a supernatural until I have found the limits of what is natural. I assume we live in a natural world, one we can gain an understanding of bit by bit by studying it, paying attention, and engaging with it closely.

CHARACTERISTICS OF SOUND BELIEFS

Beliefs I choose need to be clearly stated, make sense, and ring true to my personal experience.

IDEA OF GOD

God is not a being, but an idea. It is the ultimate expression or adjective we use for all the best we perceive and long for. The Universe is it and it is plenty! We show reverence, awe, and respect toward the Universe, toward everything around us, the world in which we are a part when we say the word God. "Thank God," "Praise God," and "Please God" are our callouts to the mysterious portions of the Universe, the majority that we don't understand and can't control, but honor.

THE UNIVERSE CONTAINS INTELLIGENCE

The pursuit of efficiency and improvement is part of the way the Universe works. In one case, via evolution, it is over time, over many, many individual lives. Alternatively, it may be an inherent force or characteristic of nature. In either case, the outcome is the same, a real tendency toward betterment. That life grows and heals and directs itself toward survival is an amazing feature.

WE ARE INDIVIDUAL AND THE WHOLE

We are individuals, and we are the Universe. Dual views of self as finite and infinite are both valid. The self fully matters, but so does our sense that we exist as an expression of the Universe. I am no worse than the other living things on the earth. I am them. At a minimum, I have the same value as the trees, the grass, and the squirrels. While I, as a single organism, will pass away, I as an extension of the Universe will continue.

LOVE AND PAIN GO TOGETHER

You can't have one without the other, and love is worth it.

LIFE ETHIC

Good behaviors are those that, if performed by all life, would make the Universe a better place for life to exist and grow. Ethics is acting such that if every life acted that way, life would be more likely to thrive.

ETHICS PRINCIPLES

I have selected six principles for behaviors in line with a Life Ethic.

- Be aware: Be mindful of others. Be conscious of the effects of your life on others. Use awareness to manage and balance the other principles.

- Be compassionate: Show sympathy for the suffering or bad luck of others. Connect emotionally to the circumstances that others are facing.

- Be generous: Give time, attention, money, help, and kindness to others. Recognize that the playing field is not equal, and opportunity is not evenly dispersed. Help with this.

- Be positive: Give others cause for hope and confidence. Leave people feeling better than before.

- Be truthful: Be honest; do not lie or deceive. Take the consequences if need be.

- Be vital: Be full of life and energy and will to persevere. Do your job. Be healthy, be smart, be as able as possible. Use your attributes and characteristics. The Universe outfitted you for what it expects and needs. Take up your space, use the resources you need, do not take more than you need. Use the self-directed part of your identity to do what you can do to live your life.

PREDETERMINED OR FREE WILL?

Everything is not predetermined. The past and the present both make up reality; both exist and are not significantly differentiated. The only difference between the reality of the past and the reality of the present is our ability to act on it. Take advantage of your present, your *now*.

13
REVISIT

Despair is the word for it. Feeling hopeless and living day to day, knowing that we've lost so much. Sickness and death, the devaluing of truth, the erosion of kindness and compassion in society that I saw the last few years weighed heavy on my mind and heart. The COVID-19 pandemic brought so much fear, loneliness, and sadness, but the pandemic was just a part of it. This plague occurred in a time already saturated with political divisiveness that verged on hatred. These recent years have been brutal.

My brother Jim is a wonderful and recurring character in this book. There are so many stories of him and our joyous times hiking and camping together. As much as I love and admire him, our relationship was not immune to the craziness of these times. We argued about politics and the pandemic, which was so painful and put our close connection to the test.

We held it together because we love each other, but it was a tough time emotionally.

I wrote most of this book during this life-sucking period. Writing was a type of therapy. I did this to find my voice and share it. There was something important I had to say about my lifelong wrestling match with these philosophical topics. First, I looked at my old writings, writings from that big day after class, and writings from my *Good Consideration* essay. I revisited them, so to speak, and nostalgia flowed. Those deep but dated words reminded me of a different time and of special people and places.

I am nostalgic by nature. Several years ago, I took Carolyn to see my old stomping grounds in Seekonk and up to the site of family lore, Mount Marcy. When I am in Schenectady, I often swing by my grandparents' house and I am comforted just seeing that it is still there. I have always loved going back to places I used to live or play. I get a little thrill thinking that I was once in the same spot. At those places, the years from that remembered boy to me now become fluid. Time somewhat disappears. Revisiting memory-filled places is like time travel.

As this book developed, I had the idea to take nostalgia one step further and go back to my original church parish, Our Lady of Mount Carmel, to visit my old church in Seekonk. I imagined entering the church, quietly taking in the scene, standing at the back, and contemplating the years that have passed. I planned to take in the church vibe and speak softly under my breath to my mom and dad, not expecting a response but just needing to honor and thank them. Would the liturgy and theology bother me? Certainly. I would have been in a swirl of conflicting feelings. Pleasant memories would clash with the supernatural focus of the Mass, but still I considered making a visit.

I checked Our Lady of Mount Carmel Church's website and saw that my prospects for visiting were not good. This was 2021, after the worst period of the pandemic, but the world was still not normal. We should probably drop the word "normal" and the phrase "return to normal" from our vocabulary.

The COVID-19 pandemic produced waves or spikes in the number of cases because of mutations, variants that held the world in a scary and isolated state for years. These variant waves had finally eased in late 2021. The church had returned to holding services. They cordoned off pews, and they expected family groups to wear masks and keep six feet of distance between others. There was a separate seating over-flow area set up in the basement, and the service was live-streamed there. While part of me wanted to visit, I decided it would not be wise. It did not feel right. If I had traveled to Seekonk and attended Mass, the big takeaways would be of the virus and the mitigat-ing behaviors everyone employed. I did not visit the church. I didn't visit later either, after COVID eased further. The service is for the faithful. Church is not meant for nonbelievers like me who want to remi-nisce.

Next, I thought of Siena. I wanted to visit the Siena College campus and recreate that scene I described at the beginning of this book. Could I conjure that same feeling of connection to the Universe all around me that occurred that afternoon after class? During COVID, the Siena College website also described various restrictions on visitation. This was so disappointing. I always felt at home there, welcomed. The prohibitions made sense, though. They had their hands full hosting students in the residences, managing classes in the teaching rooms, running the cafeteria, and guiding students through this rough COVID situation.

Fortunately, time was my friend. Many institutions significantly reduced their COVID-19 restrictions. Travel started happening again. Fear was lower, though not eliminated. Many people, including Carolyn and me, were vaccinated and boosted. In-person meetings were now regular. Life was not exactly normal, whatever that means, more of a facsimile but much better. The Siena campus was ready after more than a year since I first thought about visiting. The time was right to go back to school, so I revisited the place that meant so much to me, Siena College!

I reached out to Mike, my college roommate, to see whether he wanted to meet me. We were roommates for all four years of school, which is rare. He is a great guy. He, his wife, and daughter, all Siena graduates, came up for the weekend. Beyond that, Dr. Burkey, my primary philosophy teacher from my time at Siena, agreed to meet us that Saturday afternoon. What a couple of days we had.

That Saturday in October was fantastic in every sense. After a morning run, I drove over to the cemetery in Schenectady to visit my mom and dad's graves. It was about 8:00 a.m. The weather was clear and cool, and the dew sparkled on the grass. Everything was the same as the last time I was there, thirteen years earlier after my school's twenty-year class reunion. Time passes slower at cemeteries. Moment to moment, not much seems to change.

Standing by their graves eventually felt odd and impersonal, so I put my leather jacket on the ground and sat on it in front of the stone. I could hear maintenance vehicles and soft conversation in the distance as I tried to concentrate and open my mind at the same time. Sadness did not overcome me. In fact, gratitude and thankfulness for their love filled me. As I whispered, I smiled a little. I remembered my parents with their happiest laughing faces.

I sat on the grass for about twenty minutes. Almost nothing changed around me. I could have been there fifteen minutes or an hour, and nothing around me would have been noticeably different. I guess the words for this are "peace" and "calm." That is what I felt. Peace, calm, and deep thankfulness for their unwavering love. I miss them, but I am thankful for them too.

Leaving the cemetery, I drove by my grandparents' house, which was nearby. I was totally indulging in nostalgia on this trip. I made a quick stop, then parked across the street. My car was a black SUV, and I didn't want people to get suspicious, to think I was up to something. There is something pleasant about returning to a physical location where you once walked, played, laughed. I felt cut loose a little from 2022. The house looked similar to what I remembered from ages ago. In my mind's eye, I saw a memory of Dad and me throwing apples at each other across my grandparents' yard in an odd dodgeball kind of way. How do you not smile at that?

After a respite at the hotel, I met Mike and Isabel on the Siena campus. We walked around for a while. The school has grown and improved since the late 1980s. It is so appealing and impressive. I asked, not fully joking, "Where do I enroll?" Mike and Isabel's daughter Cheryl joined us, and we toured some more. The day was beautiful and enjoyable. After a while, I felt antsy. The time was approaching for me to do what I set out to do, recreate the scene from after that class that inspired my first writing.

I told my friends I would meet them later. My heart quickened as I looked across campus at Roger Bacon Hall and headed that way. The front of the building didn't match what I had in my head. The wide gran-ite entrance I remembered was more of a small porch. I pulled the metal door handle and opened it wide. I was under a pleasant spell until my work phone rang and I started juggling the door, my notebook, my two phones, and suddenly one phone slipped. The door closed with a crash, me inside. This all broke the peace of the moment. It was a spam call too!

Regrouping, I turned around and stepped back through the door to the outside porch. No enlightenment ideas poured through my mind this time. I looked around at the pretty scene. Thirty-five years had passed since that day after class. So much was the same, but so much life had been lived between then and now. I looked to the left, and the scene opened up. The campus lawn spread out with its inviting paths, trees, and low hills. The afternoon sun shone brightly, and the leaves showed their fall brilliance. The sky was not wispy, just pure blue today. I stood there for a moment waiting for the Universe to reveal more of its secrets.

Still waiting on the Universe, I pulled out a small journal and started writing what I was thinking and seeing. The nature of that campus area was as beautiful as I remembered it. I had a similar feeling back at the cemetery. Part of me feels as if I am the same, that nothing has changed. I'm the same person as all those years ago. It is as though I have floated down the river. Much of the journey is behind me now.

As I sat there, I picked up the sounds of far-off music. It was the song "Take It Easy" by the Eagles. That made me smile. Maybe that was my message for the day, to take it easy. I have put so much effort and hard work, for decades, into trying to figure out the big riddles of life. Maybe I should take a break and be at peace with the seeking. Who knows?

With that, I stood up and started my walk down the same path I walked decades ago toward my dorm. The buildings have changed. First, I passed the library on my left, then the dining hall, then across to the right the student union where the old library used to be. Suddenly, I heard my name. Mike was calling me. I joined my friends on the student union patio. We sat for about thirty minutes talking, laughing, and reminiscing. It was wonderful.

The last event of this marvelous day was when Dr. John Burkey joined us at a biergarten in Albany around 4:00 that afternoon. I had not seen him since my college days. He recently retired and, surprisingly, still remembered us. We all talked for a couple of hours with an easy and joyful rapport.

The next day, when I returned home, Carolyn asked me what the best moments, or highlights, were. I said there were two specific moments. One was catching sight of Mike and Isabel when they got off the elevator at the hotel on Friday evening. The last time I saw them was at our twenty-year reunion in 2009. The second highlight was seeing Dr. Burkey as he walked toward us Saturday afternoon. I am sure I glowed. My dog Bradley whimpers and whines when she reunites and meets people. I did not do that. I made no audible noises, but I was similar inside, so happy to see everyone.

Maybe the key takeaway from this revisit trip is the people. It is not the location, the campus. It isn't even the big ideas. People are at the center. From the grateful memories I felt of my loving parents to the warmth and genuineness of these kind friends, I felt embraced. The message on this trip was a human one. One filled with love, kindness, and warm appreciation. It was a weekend I will never forget.

14
CLOSING

Everyone was home! Alex and Sammy, plus a close friend and their pets, had arrived. Combined, two dogs, two cats, and five humans in our house for Christmas weekend. Yes, Christmas. You may wonder how I can celebrate Christmas. So much of this book argues against a supernatural, faith-based approach to life. Shouldn't I be against Christmas and any religious celebration? How can I celebrate Christmas when I do not believe in a God-being or the supernatural? The answer is that I enjoy certain parts. I take the best parts of Christmas—the love, the gathering of family, the satisfaction of tasty meals together, the play of our pets, nostalgia for the past, and seeds of hope for the future—and I dump the rest. I dump the reliance on miracles and super-natural forces. That is how I approach Christmas.

Friday, two days before Christmas, I layered lasagna noodles in a dish. This is one of our prized traditions. I remember my mom making the best lasagna, and so

I try to follow her recipe and emulate her technique each holiday season. When I first started making this meal ages ago, I asked her for specifics about the order of the layers. She said not to worry about the recipe or the order of the noodles, cheese, and sauce, that the ingredients were so good, the meal took care of itself. She had a point, but I still try to follow in her steps on this meal. Today, I am making it in advance, which I think makes it taste even better. This dish will go in the fridge overnight and we will eat it on Christmas Eve.

We continued with other Christmas traditions. A few days ago, Carolyn and I decorated our tree, a pre-lit artificial tree. We did not set out a manger scene as I did back in the 1970s, but I still have many of those old ornaments. I smiled as I pulled them from the tissue paper and placed them on the tree. The tissue paper was superfluous, as many of these were durable plastic ornaments.

One of these durable types that I look forward to seeing each year is an old egg-shaped ornament with a glittered-up decoupage Santa image. I made this in a grade school project from a L'eggs stocking egg. One fragile ornament we handle with care is a huge green ornament that has been handed down over several generations from my father's family from Germany. Then there are a bunch of cool ornaments that Sammy and Alex gave Carolyn. My favorites are the many special ornaments that mark joys and milestones of Carolyn's and my life together—travel destinations, events, or scenes with the year noted on the back.

We did not go to midnight Mass, nor any Mass. There was no Advent wreath with special candles counting down to the birth of Jesus, but we had regular candles that gave the room that soft glow. I didn't notice any prayer, at least anything formally recited, but I heard lots of laughter and the clinking of glasses. There was Christmas music and our favorite shows and seasonal movies. You might say this was a secular Christmas, and you would be right, but I would not want that to be confused with a commercial Christmas. We kept gifts to a minimum, mostly holding to what could fit in a stocking. This Christmas weekend was about family love, taking a break from the hectic world, and making happy memories together.

One Christmas morning when I was a child, I got my dad's OK and began ringing a set of sleigh bells as loud as I could to wake my sleeping brothers and sister. I loved being that annoying Christmas angel clanging away for an early morning start to our festival of presents. No one else liked it. This year I did not ring any bells. I just stopped being quiet in the kitchen, and by 9:00 a.m. the clattering was at a normal level and soon everyone was around. We opened presents and talked about the reasons for each, and the just-perfect finds. We watched the dogs rip wrappers. It was as idyllic as it sounds.

What do you think of my Christmas compromise? Is it OK? Yes, I think so. Why would I hate Christmas?

My personality and memories are rich with Christmas experiences. It is easy to want black and white, stark differences between things, toggle switches between this or that, such as no Christian faith means no Christmas to enjoy. Life may be more of a dimmer switch than a toggle one. Life is often more nuanced, and Christmas is one of these times. Flipping the switch of Christmas to Off would have been difficult and not beneficial. Celebrating with loved ones in a peaceful, warm, safe environment is truly something that, if done by everyone, would make the world a better place for life to exist and grow. Much more so than if I coldly railed against this semireligious day because of its reliance on the supernatural.

My natural-not-supernatural-oriented philosophy is sometimes tricky to live with. Christmas is a good example. We can honor our intellectual ideas and still make choices about how to live in a religiously oriented society. Our past does not bind us, but it shapes us. We can subtly shift our way of living to honor our upbringing, our past, while aligning more fully with our emerging values and intellectual views. I think it is worth the effort.

You may conclude that I appear stuck in that same place I was decades ago, trying to cling to the familiar while exploring new ideas. That is not correct. I have explored ideas and I love what I have produced, but I have found that ideas need to fit with my whole person to become my beliefs. They need to align with me in deep ways, ways that encompass the gifts of my loved ones and my life experiences.

Fortunately, this is doable. I mentioned my view of God as the meta-idea, an expression, not a noun. This was a way to hold on to the reverence and awe for the Universe that was forged in me early in life while dropping the idea of a supernatural God. Similarly, I can hear people talk about other supernatural words and I don't need to argue away their views. I can translate their words into expressions of fear and helplessness in the face of a Universe we barely understand. No need to fight about supernatural words that I can imagine differently, in ways more consistent with my philosophy.

This works. I can translate supernatural terms into rich meanings that express human emotions of the Universe. Someone says "Please God" and I hear their human, emotional plea, a wish expressed to the Universe because that is all they can do. There is so much out of our control. That is something I can relate to. I hear "Praise God" and I hear the reverence those words express about the amazing Universe. I can sure relate to that too. I hear "Thank God" and I hear gratitude toward the Universe that gave us our individual lives and nurtures us daily.

I imagine a room with several people, and each one says "Please God" softly to themselves under their breath as they wish something great for themselves or others. One may be directing this plea to a Catholic God, one to the God of the Hebrew faith, one to the

Muslim God; maybe others whisper hopeful prayers to many gods in so many belief systems. Each person is making a request, and I empathize with them. I feel these same feelings. My wishes and hopes are real, as are theirs. There is so much out of our control and so much we wish would happen to our loved ones and to us. Many use the word God for this. God is a label many people use for the powers beyond our understanding or control. Instead of calling to a God-being, I direct my hope to the Universe. We are a lot alike. I am sure there are natural powers out there way beyond my understanding. The difference is, I will not call these supernatural. The natural world is amazing and enough.

There is no need to argue about God or the super-natural. We can understand these loaded words as expressions of emotion, longing, loss, fear, or appre-ciation. We can hold our critical conversations to the workings of the Universe while expressing our human doubts and fears of so much that is unknown and out of our control. Let's bring our full humanity, use the word God, but own that it says something about our outlook on a natural Universe. Let's not pretend we have all the answers and that these answers derive from an indescribable, supernatural noun.

* * *

Building my own beliefs is a monumental and con-tinuing challenge. One that never ends. Even now, with so much spelled out here, my beliefs are still a work in process. I don't want to imply that this philosophy is the truth of reality. It is my current view and I will keep working on it, challenging it for clarity, reasonableness, and fit.

The approach to developing a philosophy is as important as the philosophy itself. The value in *Natural Wonders* is not in the specifics of the beliefs themselves, it is in how I developed them. I strove for clarity and reasonability in the ideas and then bounced those ideas against my personal experience. Using this process made the views open and explainable to others. I built my ideas by hand, brick by brick, point by point, each idea bound with the mortar of my life experiences. This is a vast difference from claiming some divine direct-access answers for the riddles of the Universe.

It is possible to live without the concept of the supernatural. We can see ourselves as finite beings and as pieces of the whole. We can find morality in how we interact with one another and our environments instead of vague promises of paradise in an afterlife. It is possible to live ethically by evaluating our actions and asking what the world would look like if everyone acted that way.

Rather than rely on words from ancient texts, we can blend the earned wisdom of our experiences with the fruits of our thinking. We all can choose what to believe through honest introspection, consideration, and communication. If humanity had taken the non-religious route generations ago, had chosen clarity, reason, and personal experience over comforting myths of supernatural powers, we would be so much better today, and humanity could feel collective pride rather than embarrassment and shame for how we have lived and what we have done to one another for centuries.

I think it is not too late. The world feels so fractured and conflicted, but in many ways, it has never been smaller or more connected. Information is so accessible. Exposure to other people and ideas is readily available. Humanity can be better, and we can develop a world that is more open to approaches like the one I described here. We can get there one idea at a time, each idea offered gently and honestly, all intending to build a view or paradigm that supports life. For us, our children, and generations to come, let's try!

15

DISCUSSION

How do you think your parents would view your philosophy and *Natural Wonders*?

First, they may not have wanted to read it. They may not have wanted to hear anything about it. If they had read it and we talked about it, I think they would eventually have been OK with it. Their responses would have been unique to each parent. Mom was so love focused. If she had realized that love is essentially what I am advocating with the ethics layer cake, she would have been accepting. She would have been worried about my soul and that I did not go to church. Maybe she wouldn't understand why I needed to go my own way, but she would have remained kind. Dad would have been torn. On the one hand, he would have appreciated the effort and persistence. He would have acknowledged the accomplishment of writing this. He, like my mom, was devout and would have been concerned for my soul, my eventual judgment day. Overall, I think he would have understood. They probably would not have ostracized me, but this would have been an uncomfortable point between us.

Do you wish you never had that natural and supernatural idea back then in college?

What if someone had stopped me as I left that building and distracted me? What if I had a cell phone in my hand and stared at that rather than the natural scene? Obviously, cell phones did not exist back then, so I dodged that potential outcome. In both cases, I may never have had that inspired walk and come up with that initial big idea. Somehow, I think I would have ended up in the same place. The forces eroding my faith and spurring on my thoughts then were real. These forces would have found their way to action. Do I regret it? My life would have been easier without the natural and supernatural key idea. It probably would be simpler, but no, I don't think it would be better. If I had stayed with the church, then I would have endorsed so much that wasn't me. No, I do not wish that afternoon had been different.

Are you concerned about how you will be viewed, perhaps distanced from the religious people in your life?

Yes, I am. There are many people I love and respect who are Catholic and I am concerned that when they read this, or hear about it, they will find it disturbing. They will find that they don't know me as well as they thought. This is on me. Up to this point, I have not shared my views very much. They may not want me around anymore, or this material could insult or hurt them. I call out strongly against faith-based beliefs, and they could see this as an attack on them. There may be painful relationship consequences of this book for me. Conversely, this essay may reach some people positively and help them feel better about how they are dealing with their own personal faith and religious questions.

What do you think are the best and weakest points in the book?

Obviously, the "everything is natural" idea is the cornerstone. This idea has been with me for thirty-five years and feels increasingly true. The Life Ethic is strong too. I am proud of that. Also, the "individual and Universe" idea as being two views of the same thing is interesting. Some would call this New Age or woo-woo, being one with the Universe, but it makes sense and rings true. The six ethical principles are good and reflect my views and values, but anyone could come up with six principles of their own. There is nothing necessary or essential to these specific six. They are like an honor society of ideas or inductees in my Ethical Principles Hall of Fame.

One other point I am proud of is the three-pronged criteria I settled on for forming a belief: clear, reasonable, and experiential fit. This is pretty strong. Doubting and searching while in college is common, but for me, I looked at nature and at my experiences rather than outside experts or thought leaders. I probably could have saved lots of time and trouble if I read more and contemplated less, but I wanted this philosophy to be mine, to reflect as much as possible my personal synthesis of thinking and living. I am proud of the approach.

The weakest point is not so weak as it is sad. It hurt when I gave up on the possibility of believing in a supernatural God-being. It had to be, but I felt the loss. This is the reason I use the words "reverence," "respect," and "awe" so much. As a boy, I revered God and am trying to hold on to portions of that outlook. I now think of God as a human-made idea, not a being. God is the ultimate expression or adjective we use for all the best we perceive and desire for ourselves and others.

Considering that you do not believe in a supernatural God or even a natural God-being, would you describe yourself as an atheist?

I probably fit into that category, but the word doesn't feel comfortable. The word does not capture the awe-filled outlook on the Universe I am trying to convey. This is the view that the Universe itself is fully amazing. The Universe is like divinity itself. The reason identifying as atheist bothers me is that I associate it with a disregard for the magic-like wonders of the Universe. It seems devoid of brilliance and disrespects the awesomeness and ridiculously amazing characteristics of everything we see, touch, and hear around us.

The leap to think of God as an expression was huge. God is an idea, an idea we can apply to the highest and deepest elements of our human existence and awareness. It is a descriptor, an adjective, not a noun. It says something about how we see existence, not what exists or does not exist. In this way, I feel I have brought the idea of God along with me rather than banished it. God is a little like a mirror in that the meaning reflects us and our situation when we call on that word.

What has it been like writing *Natural Wonders*?

It has been much more challenging than I expected. It has probably been the lowest-yielding activity I ever took on. By that, I mean the number of hours and effort put in for the amount of quality output. It has been a passionate hobby more than anything. I worked on this mostly nights and weekends. Sometimes I would go a few weeks without writing, then I would have a flurry of activity. I have a stack of printed revisions on my shelf and countless versions of files on my computer.

I value this process, though. The act of writing generated innovative ideas and helped me clarify existing ones. Writing a work like this is not central to my career. It is not in the sweet spot of my skill set, but it has been rewarding and even fun. In some ways, I think of it as my life's work. I hope to continue developing these ideas and expressing them to the best of my ability in the future.

When did you write *Natural Wonders*, and how long has it taken?

The ideas came at a glacial pace. I wrote those natural and supernatural words back in 1988. I wrote the *Good Consideration* essay in 1999. About ten years ago, I returned to thinking about philosophy and writing about what I was thinking. I guess I started pulling all this together and writing *Natural Wonders* in 2019, just before COVID-19 hit. I wrote most of the new material during COVID times, so it has taken me approximately four years to pull this full book together. The deepest, darkest days of COVID, which also overlapped with polarizing politics, were so depressing and so challenging. This book was a creative outlet and a tremendous help during those hard days in 2020 and 2021.

The Siena-era notebook and *Good Consideration* were writings you kept mostly to yourself. What made you decide to publish *Natural Wonders*?

First, I wanted to write a more comprehensive story of my life with philosophy, not just a treatise on philosophical points. I wanted to put my ideas into context. Second, I think many people are unsure how to reconcile their raised-in faith with new ideas they are thinking. I felt I could share my pain and struggle with this. I thought by expressing my internal conflict and how I eventually navigated that conflict, I might help others. Last, I think we need fresh ideas on ethics that are grounded in the natural. I really wanted to share the Life Ethic idea with others.

What do you think of your early church experiences? Were you glad your family raised you in the Catholic Church?

I truly value the Catholic education and values that my parents gave me. I think when adults pause from their daily duties and pressures and take time out to revere something big, bigger than the daily grind, that is wonderful. This does not need to happen in a church. We probably could have used less formal natural settings with some focused contemplative time, and that may have provided the same benefit. I think exposure to the idea of God as a child made me a better person. This helped me see beyond my nose and my immediate wants. If this could have evolved and opened up as I grew, then maybe the conflict that tormented me as a young adult would have eased. If we had a little less faith and a little more wonder, maybe I could have avoided that pain and guilt. That Siena afternoon insight would have been the next normal step for me rather than a dangerous and hurtful leap.

Any parting thoughts or comments?

Imagine a world in which non-supernatural, Universe-oriented principles replaced religion in society. Can you imagine if civilization did not spend so much time and energy generating so much hate and violence because of religious differences? Think of the lively debates and thoughts and experiences that could have advanced the conversation around morality and our role in the Universe. We could be so much further along as a society if these conversations avoided supernatural assumptions and related dogma. Think of what the world would be now if we had spent the last few thousand years considering, peacefully evaluating, and discussing ideas grounded in the natural world, allowing for differences but never abandoning reason and experience for fable and myth. We would have a healthier, kinder world. Maybe it's not too late.

ACKNOWLEDGMENTS

This book is a product of decades of living and wondering. I have spent so many hours with my head in the clouds, trying to figure life out. In the end, people in my life made the difference. You influenced me, taught me lessons, and encouraged me. You challenged me and educated me by the example you set. You are my family, friends, teachers, supervisors at work, even acquaintances. So many kind and wise people have filled my life and helped me wonder about life's mysteries.

That is not to slight my dog, Bradley. She is a walking, sniffing example of the wonders of the Universe wrapped in black fur. Watching her has inspired me to see more directly the amazing aspects of the Universe playing out by my side. To twist my phrase, if everyone behaved like Bradley, the world would be a better place.

As I wrote this over the last four years, through rough times as COVID raged, waned, and raged again, Carolyn has been the constant source of love and kindness. She read the roughest early versions of this book, plus the less rough but still painful mid-versions of this book, and gently helped me improve the clarity and tone. Her advice helped me lean more toward a conversational style in my writing, to say or dig for more, with less of that term paper voice that is my tendency. We hashed out ideas together, and her take on life has inspired me. This book would not exist without her.

I want to mention two others who contributed and motivated me. Mike Clemens, my friend and Siena College roommate, read a copy of the manuscript while on vacation and, like days of old, sent me several helpful, challenging ideas and insights. In addition, our college philosophy professor, Dr. John Burkey, also read a draft of the book and he encouraged me, which meant so much.

Last, thanks to David Wogahn and the team at AuthorImprints for facilitating this self-publishing effort. Particular thanks to Diane Rush for her terrific editing work. Beyond technical corrections, she understood what I was trying to say and suggested changes to make it simpler and more impactful. Thank you!

ABOUT THE AUTHOR

Bob Wilhelm is a career management accounting professional, a longtime paper industry finance leader who has served as vice president for two public companies in the industry. For over thirty years, Bob has worked in mill towns and large cities, providing financial analysis and partnering with stakeholders to support manufacturing business goals.

Besides his management accounting interests and career, Bob has a love of ideas and philosophy. *Natural Wonders* is his debut work on these big ideas. You can find out more about Bob on his website, bwilhelmideas.com. Bob lives with his wife, Carolyn, and dog, Bradley, in Chattanooga, Tennessee.

www.ingramcontent.com/pod-product-compliance
Lightning Source LLC
Chambersburg PA
CBHW020237130626
46549CB00005B/1931